Editor

Craig Donnellan

Independence

Educational Publishers

Cambridge

First published by Independence
PO Box 295
Cambridge CB1 3XP

© Craig Donnellan 1996

British Library Cataloguing in Publication Data
Biotechnology – Friend or Foe? – (Issues for the Nineties Series)
I. Donnellan, Craig II. Series
660.6

I. Donnellan, Craig
ISBN 1 872995 80 2

Printed in Great Britain
at Leicester Printers Ltd
Leicester

Typeset by
Martyn Lusher Artwork, Cambridge

Cover
The illustration on the front cover is by
Anthony Haythornthwaite / Folio Collective.

CONTENTS

Chapter One: Recent developments

Chapter Two: Right or wrong?

Introduction

Biotechnology – Friend or Foe? is the twelfth volume in the series: **Issues For The Nineties**. The aim of this series is to offer up-to-date information about important issues in our world.

Biotechnology – Friend or Foe? gives an overview of recent developments and examines the ethical debate. The information comes from a wide variety of sources and includes:

Government reports and statistics
Newspaper reports and features
Magazine articles and surveys
Literature from lobby groups
and charitable organisations.

It is hoped that, as you read about the many aspects of the issues explored in this book, you will critically evaluate the information presented. It is important that you decide whether you are being presented with facts or opinions. Does the writer give a biased or an unbiased report? If an opinion is being expressed, do you agree with the writer?

Biotechnology – Friend or Foe? offers a useful starting-point for those who need convenient access to information about the many issues involved. However, it is only a starting-point. At the back of the book is a list of organisations which you may want to contact for further information.

*****

Dispelling the monster myth

Biotechnology – separating science from fiction

Public perception of biotechnology is derived from distorted media coverage, science fiction and the literature of the grotesque rather than hard, scientific fact, according to Professor Graham Street of the University of Teesside. In his professorial lecture this week he attempted to redress the balance and dispel some of the myths. Chris Kirkham talked to him about the struggle to improve biotechnology's public image

It was the kind of story likely to be ignored by the tabloids and maybe given a few column inches in some of the 'quality' press. Researchers in biotechnology had discovered a way to ensure that all the tomatoes in a given crop would ripen on the same day. This would obviously help the farmer in harvesting the crop and subsequently reduce delays in getting the tomatoes on to the market stalls and supermarket displays. A small step forward for science, agriculture and salad-eating mankind?

Well, not the way *The Daily Telegraph* reported it. 'Frankenstein's Tomatoes' blared the headline, an image which evokes concepts such as 'science against nature', 'monster' and 'genetic engineering'.

It was this kind of reportage with regard to biotechnological advances that most annoyed Graham Street. It's well known that despite successful recent ventures into the public domain, like Set 7, science and scientists are viewed with a great deal of suspicion by the British public. His professorial lecture, a few days ago, attempted to place biotechnology firmly within a distinguished scientific tradition as well as correcting a few misconceptions.

What makes Professor Street's arguments on behalf of his discipline so persuasive is the sheer range of his allusions encompassing literature, Hollywood and pre-history.

> ## 'Too often biotechnology is reported with this Frankenstein tag, as if it's some kind of monster'

He illustrates his main points with blown-up cartoons of Disney's *Alice in Wonderland*, drinking a curious potion and swelling up to fill a house or shrinking to the size of a mouse. Lewis Carroll's vivid imagination or an early indication of how growth hormones can be manipulated? And what of Frankenstein's monster? Genetic engineering gone mad, or what?

It's a crowd-pleasing tactic that carries a serious message 'Biotechnology is the application of biological organisms, systems or processes to manufacturing and service industries, and as such it has positive benefits for mankind. For example, we can produce bacteria which can be sprayed on to crops, preventing them from freezing. That's obviously good for farmers, and it's good for those people who need a supply of fresh food in different seasons. But too often it's reported with this Frankenstein tag, as some sort of monster. And it's that sort of image I want to get rid of.'

Professor Street says he's amazed how often this 'monster' image is

used by journalists seeking to sensationalise a scientific development and cause spurious controversy. 'I saw a cartoon from Germany illustrating a story about a company which had been stopped from producing insulin because of doubts about the process used. The cartoon portrayed Gulliver, tied down by the Lilliputians, but Gulliver was drawn as Frankenstein's monster. Now, quite obviously, the implication was that the ropes were preventing a monster from getting loose. I was annoyed because not only was this representation scientifically inaccurate – we all know how important insulin is – but the literary source was misused: when Gulliver freed himself from the ropes he actually saved Lilliput from its enemies – he was a saviour, not a destroyer.'

The professor's lecture, interestingly enough, contained a historical perspective of its own. He cited cheese production in 3500 BC as a natural food process which has been brought into the 21st century through recent developments in bio-process engineering.

'The irony is that if you use biotechnology for people's health, it's good, but if you use it in food production, somehow it isn't and food companies have a lot more difficulty getting it accepted.'

And a personal irony for this campaigner is that tomatoes seemed to have featured prominently in his career. The man incensed by the 'Frankenstein's Tomatoes' headline was once involved in making tomato ketchup for Heinz. Tomatoes grown in Portugal were shipped over to Britain, pulped into paste and then processed into the user-friendly ketchup. He also helped developed Heinz's successful range of baby foods. That was in the sixties before academic prospects beckoned and he joined the Department of Biochemical Engineering at University College, London, working on enzyme technology. He migrated north to Teesside in 1973 and has remained there ever since.

Today, he carries out research on process integration, whilst acting as lobbyist for his own particular branch of science.

'Biotechnology has a direct

'Frankenstein's Tomatoes' blared the headline

impact on the quality of human, animal and plant life. Before 1980, it was very much an individuals' discipline, most of the advances came from individual scientists pursuing their own theories. Then, in 1980,

the Spinks Report was produced, which was a turning-point in the development of biotechnology as an internationally recognised technology of major significance. After this report, it became embedded in economic development.'

Scientific recognition has to be followed by public acceptance, he says. 'I want a public debate examining how some biotechnological discoveries are presented to and understood by the world at large.'

The professorial lecture was one stage in the process of stimulating that debate. The next step, presumably, is for scientists like Graham Street to start writing their own press coverage, eliminating such tired journalistic clichés as the Frankenstein image once and for all. Watch this space.

© University Life
August, 1995

Knowledge of biotechnology

How much do you know about biotechnology?

We asked people how much they would say that they knew about biotechnology. We found that only one-third of adults in Great Britain claimed to have any knowledge at all; two-thirds of adults knew nothing at all about biotechnology or have never heard of it.

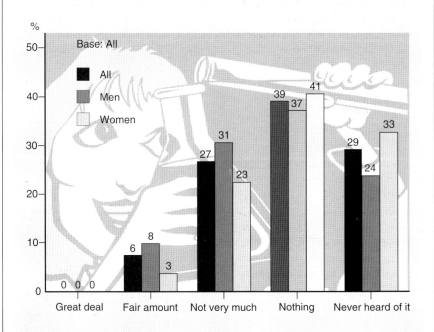

	Great deal	Fair amount	Not very much	Nothing	Never heard of it
All	0	6	27	39	29
Men	0	8	31	37	24
Women	0	3	23	41	33

● The above is an extract from *Consumers and Biotechnology*, a report on research conducted for the Food and Drink Federation. See page 39 for address details.

© The Food and Drink Federation
September, 1995

Genes and mankind

For thousands of years, mankind has wondered about the mysterious processes that direct our growth and development. What is it that could possibly determine the colour of a person's hair, people asked – or our eyes, or skin? And what decides if a child is going to grow up to be short or tall, healthy or sickly, stout or slim – or be a boy or a girl, for that matter?

Today we know the basic answer. Each of us has a complement of between 50,000 to 100,000 genes contained in bundles, that are known as chromosomes, and which lie coiled within the cells that make up our tissue and organs. These genes control the manufacture of the proteins that are our bodies' chemical tools and building blocks. They determine, for example, the colour of our eyes, hair and skin – and our sex.

The medicine of tomorrow

At present we know the position and structure of only a few thousand human genes. The Human Genome Project aims to trace every single member of our gene system (which is called the human genome) and to assign each gene to its proper place on its appropriate chromosome. This process is known as mapping.

Scientists intend to unravel the structure of each gene (a task called sequencing) and determine the composition of its corresponding protein and its role within our bodies.

Researchers will therefore gain unprecedented knowledge about human physiology and the multitude of proteins and hormones that constantly interact during our body's normal functioning. We will learn about individual susceptibilities to disease, and will be able to target these for early remedial, preventative treatments. This source of information will also be applied to create new drugs and other medicines

Imperial Cancer
Research Fund

to counteract cancers, heart diseases, immune disorders and other illnesses. Most pharmaceuticals will be made this way next century.

In addition, we will gain new insights into the working of the mind, learn about the genetic relatedness of the different human races and create new forensic techniques like those involved in genetic fingerprinting.

It is a highly ambitious task. Nevertheless, scientists are confident that, in this way, they can eventually unravel the complex biological processes that go together to make 'a piece of work' like man.

The Human Genome Project

The Human Genome Project has been described as biology's equivalent of the Apollo Moon programme and it is estimated the undertaking will cost $2 billion to complete – probably by the beginning of the next century.

Unlike other big science enterprises, however, there is no central laboratory or research block where the project is administered and implemented. Instead, individual nations have set up their own programmes for mapping and sequencing genes, and the project's different tasks and components are shared out on a largely informal basis between scientists working at these various centres.

These different activities are co-ordinated informally by an international group of scientists known as the Human Genome Organisation (Hugo) which has been created to supervise the world's mapping and sequencing activities and to ensure there is no duplication of effort between different countries.

● The above is an extract from the publication *Genes and Mankind*, available from the Imperial Cancer Research Fund. See page 39 for address details.

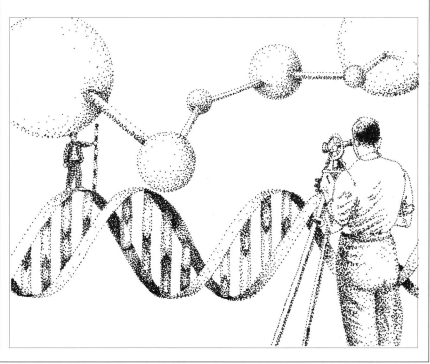

Biotechnology offers a safer, more secure world

Widespread fears that safeguards already in place are inadequate are probably based on ignorance

By David Richardson

Biotechnology designed to produce genetically modified organisms via the manipulation of deoxyribonucleic acid is not just a mouthful – it is beyond the wit of most people to comprehend.

Reduce that acid to its initials, DNA, and its meaning becomes slightly more accessible to the average person. DNA is, after all, constantly being quoted as a means of solving violent crime through genetic fingerprinting. And most of us, I suppose, are vaguely aware that it has something to do with our bodily make-up and with food and farming.

But multi-syllabic words and scientific jargon are a big turn-off for most people, and as we do not understand them we tend to fear the techniques they describe. They conjure up images of bespectacled boffins in white coats and dangerous-looking laboratories. I confess to having had some of those same fears until the commonplace nature of biotechnology in everyday foods was explained to me.

I am assured, for instance, that it is possible to extract the DNA from an onion using table salt, washing-up liquid, a normal household liquidiser, a coffee filter and very little else. Furthermore, it can be done in any kitchen or, as is already happening, in third-form school chemistry classes

Not all of those people who defy concern over cholesterol and eat cheese may be aware that the traditional way to promote the initial curdling of milk is to add a small quantity of rennet, an enzyme extracted from a calf's stomach. Biotechnology has now made it possible to produce an exact copy of chymosin, the necessary enzyme, which is indistinguishable from the original in both make-up and function, and, following approval by the UK Government's Advisory Committee on Novel Foods and Processes, it is increasingly being used in cheesemaking, much to the delight, I imagine, of the animal welfare lobby.

> **Given proper regulation and controls, the new technology is likely to produce a safer, more secure and more environment-friendly world**

Other foods and drinks whose production involves the use of living organisms, like yeast – such things as bread and beer – will also soon benefit from improved versions of raw material that are the result of biotechnology.

My own particular interest, however, is in the field of plant breeding. In the past – and it has been going on for centuries – the development of improved varieties has been done by the selection of desirable characteristics in individual plants and crossing them with one another in the hope that the result would be favourable.

In recent years, however, it has become possible to identify the qualities required from DNA analysis and achieve more accuracy in the breeding process. Plant breeders can now select far more specifically than before for such things as milling quality in wheat; resistance to debilitating fungal disease; tolerance to certain pests; and the ability to yield well with lower levels of fertiliser.

Ultimately, for it still takes many years for these characteristics to be fixed and for the resulting seed to be multiplied to sufficient quantity for it to be made widely available, this

WHAT'S IN THIS TOMATO?

Ken Pyne

work will lead to crop varieties that will require lower inputs of chemicals and fertilisers and therefore be more environmentally friendly. It will also open new doors for agriculture.

Take oilseed rape, for instance. Genetic manipulation, which will make it one of the most versatile crops in the world, is well advanced. By modifying the gene mix for different purposes, scientists are already confident that the oils produced by the different strains they are developing can become general purpose, environment-friendly, feed stocks for industry.

It could not only be used for cooking and lubrication, as at present, but also for the manufacture of plastics, polymers, pharmaceuticals, inks, detergents, nylon, cosmetics and probably many more. And, unlike the mainly fossil-based raw materials used for those processes at present, oilseed rape would amount to a renewable resource.

Scientists say that biotechnology will be our only hope as the population of the world doubles during the next 50 years. That to have any chance of putting food into those new mouths and to be able to continue to enjoy the conveniences of modern life, it is vital that the developments they can foresee continue to be introduced.

But 20th-century successors to the Luddites see dangers. Their fears, as mine were, are probably based on ignorance. They are not satisfied that the mass of safeguards already in place will protect them from some horror being released into the environment – fears which I have been persuaded are groundless.

The Government's response is to organise a Consensus Conference of interested but uninvolved people to assess the evidence during the coming autumn and come to conclusions in November.

It is a welcome and appropriate step, which I for one hope will promote a public debate in which some of the mystique and misunderstanding about biotechnology will be dispelled.

Given proper regulation and controls, the new technology is likely to produce a safer, more secure and more environment-friendly world.

Attitudes towards biotechnology

We asked people what, if any, they thought might be the benefits of biotechnology. Respondents were not prompted and answered in their own words.

Respondents identified three main areas of benefits:
- medical benefits, mentioned by 30% of all adults
- environmental benefits, mentioned by 10% of adults
- food-related benefits, mentioned by 46% – nearly half of all adults.

Food-related benefits were split into three groups:
- benefits connected with food taste, and nutritional quality (better food)
- benefits to do with the supply of food, including better availability and longer life (longer-lasting food)
- cheaper food

The most commonly mentioned 'other' benefit was treatment of animal disease.

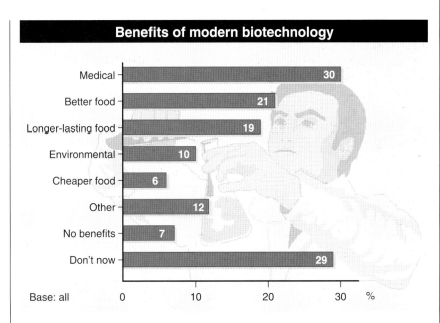

Benefits of modern biotechnology

	%
Medical	30
Better food	21
Longer-lasting food	19
Environmental	10
Cheaper food	6
Other	12
No benefits	7
Don't now	29

Base: all

Those respondents on a vegetarian diet, or who eat fish but no meat, are more likely than average to see no benefits of modern biotechnology (18% and 15% respectively).

Respondents who know about biotechnology are significantly more likely than average to name benefits of biotechnology, and are less likely than average to say that there are no benefits.

- The above is an extract from *Consumers and Biotechnology*, a report on research conducted for the Food and Drink Federation. See page 39 for address details.

The benefits of biotechnology

foodfuture

I. Plants

Fewer crops lost
Biotechnology could be used to help reduce losses to our food supplies. For example:

Disease and pest resistance
Current projects, involving genetic modification, at different stages of development aim to produce:

- Potatoes able to resist the Colorado beetle;
- Plants able to resist the 'cucumber mosaic virus' which attacks cucumber, lettuce, tomatoes, peppers and other horticultural crops;
- Fruit trees and strawberries protected from the codling moth and vine weevil;
- Crops including apple, potato, maize, cotton, rice and tomato plants resistant to insect attack;
- A viral-resistant variety of crookneck squash which could save large parts of the USA harvest;
- Plants able to resist fungal attack and bacterial disease;
- Sweet potato plants able to resist the 'feathery mottle virus' which often ruins two-thirds of the African sweet potato harvest.

Disease diagnosis
Crop diseases are difficult to spot, especially in their early stages. Diagnostic kits, utilising biotechnology, will help farmers tell whether or not their crops are infected so that they spray only when absolutely necessary.

Weed control
Weeds are another threat to our food crops, but killing the weeds can also kill the crops. Plants have now been developed which will tolerate certain herbicides, which means the weeds die but not the crops. This should lead to a reduction in the use of environmentally unfriendly herbicides which are being replaced by more benign alternatives, and save the energy and cost of repeated crop spraying.

Feeding the world
Although we seem to have more food available than ever before feeding everyone in the world is still a huge challenge:

- By the year 2000 world consumption of wheat, rice, maize, barley and other crops could be over two billion tonnes a year. That's an increase of 25% compared with today.
- During the past 50 years world population has doubled and during the next 50 it will double again. By the year 2040 there could be nearly 10,000 million people to feed.

Ultimately, feeding the world requires political solutions, but biotechnology could also help by reducing crop losses and improving and increasing food supplies.

Improved nutritional value

Higher-protein foods
Lack of protein is a major cause of malnutrition in many countries of the world. Biotechnology could be used to produce palatable high-protein crops. For example:

- Transferring genetic traits from pea plants to produce a higher-protein rice.

Modified fat foods
Corn, soyabeans, oilseed rape and other oil crops could be modified to alter their saturated fat content.

A potato with a higher starch content would absorb less oil during frying, providing an alternative method of producing lower fat products such as chips and crisps.

Higher-vitamin fruit and veg
Some fruits and vegetables could be adapted to contain higher levels of nutrients, for example, vitamins C and E. Current research suggests these changes could offer some protection against chronic diseases such as certain cancers and heart disease.

Longer-lasting fruit and veg
Genetic modification to slow down softening will provide fruits that last longer. Flavr Savr® tomatoes with this characteristic are already on sale in the USA. Slow-softening apples, raspberries and melon have also been produced and this benefit is likely to be transferable to other fruit and vegetable crops including bananas, pineapples, sweet peppers, peaches, nectarines, mangoes and strawberries.

How is it done?

The Flavr Savr® tomato is the first genetically modified whole food on the market in the USA. Tomatoes and soft fruits are usually picked while still under-ripe so that they remain firm during transportation. The modified tomatoes have had their softening gene 'switched off'. This means they can ripen on the vine until they have their full flavour and colour and still remain firm after harvesting. This should provide greater flexibility during transport and handling and give more choice to the consumer.

A copy is made of the gene responsible for the softening enzyme...and turned round so that it blocks the message that switches on the softening process

Resulting in slower-softening tomatoes...and so less waste.

Possible future developments

Drought resistance

Drought resistance in plants would enable farmers to extend both the growing season and number of places where crops could grow. This is not just a problem in hotter countries. Water availability is a limiting factor nearly everywhere plants are grown.

Nitrogen fixing

Plants need nitrogen to grow. Certain bacteria found in the roots of peas and beans can take nitrogen from the air and convert or 'fix' it for use in plant growth. Scientists are trying to use genetic modification so that these bacteria can live in the roots of cereal crops to provide a ready-made source of fertiliser. This could be cheaper and more environmentally friendly than the fertilisers we use today.

Frost damage

Frost damage can ruin many crops. Work is underway to produce plants with an inbuilt mechanism to help fight frost damage. One possibility would involve utilising the gene in fish which enables them to tolerate extreme cold. However, the prospect of copying and transferring 'animal' genes to plants is controversial. It remains to be seen whether or not this would be acceptable to the public.

II. Micro-organisms

Throughout the ages, micro-organisms such as moulds and yeasts have been used to create many different foods and drinks. For example, moulds cause the blue veins in Stilton and Gorgonzola cheese. Genetically modified micro-organisms could offer many further benefits in food production. For example:

Vegetarian cheese

The genetic information for the chymosin enzyme in calf rennet (which causes the milk-clotting reaction) has been identified and copied into yeast cells. These modified micro-organisms produce pure chymosin which is identical to the animal enzyme. This means cheese can now be made without the need to use animal rennet.

III. Farm animals

Genetic modification in the animal world is much less developed than in the plant world. It is also far more controversial. Subject to the controversy being resolved, modern biotechnology could bring a number of benefits, not just for mankind but also for the animals. For example:

Vaccines

Genetically modified vaccines are being developed to protect cattle, pigs and poultry against a variety of serious diseases.

Disease diagnosis

When vets take samples from sick animals it can take days for them to be analysed. In future, problems will be analysed on the spot with diagnostic kits developed with biotechnology.

Reduced stress

Some pigs suffer from porcine stress syndrome (PSS), which causes distress for the animal and affects meat quality. The syndrome has been traced to a specific genetic mutation. A DNA test has been developed to identify the carriers so that breeders will be able to eliminate the condition.

Other benefits

In the future, it could be possible to improve the quality of meat, milk and wool and enhance resistance to disease. Some of the genes that control these traits have already been identified. However, these applications are among the more controversial.

BST – on hold

Bacteria have been genetically modified to provide Bovine somatotropin (BST), a bovine *growth hormone* which can increase milk production by almost a quarter. However, the use of BST raised some controversial ethical, welfare and economic questions and a moratorium on the use of BST was imposed in the European Union until the year 2000. It remains to be seen if consumers find BST use acceptable thereafter.

● The above is an extract from *Food for our future – Food and biotechnology*, produced by the Food and Drink Federation. See page 39 for address details.

Genetic modification of major crops – summary of current developments

Crop	Potential Benefit
Maize	insect resistance, herbicide tolerance
Potato	virus resistance, insect resistance, higher starch content
Soyabean	virus resistance, improved nutritional composition, herbicide tolerance
Oilseed rape	modified oil composition, herbicide tolerance
Brassicas	pest resistance
Raspberries	slow ripening
Melon	slow ripening
Wheat	herbicide tolerance, modified starch types
Sunflower	modified oil composition
Salad crops	insect resistance, longer shelf-life
Apples	disease resistance, slow ripening

Gene therapy and cancer research

From the Imperial Cancer Research Fund

Imperial Cancer Research Fund

Gene therapy may soon be used as a novel treatment for malignant melanoma and Imperial Cancer Research Fund scientists are hoping to gain final approval to begin initial work with patients by the end of the year.

That's the theme of a lecture which Professor Ian Hart, Dimbleby Professor of Cancer Research at St Thomas' Hospital, London, gave to the Association of Medical Research Charities' 'From Bench to Bedside' conference on 5th September.

Professor Ian Hart, along with a representative from the National Heart and Lung Institute, spoke on 'From Mouse to Man – Gene Therapy for Cancer and Cystic Fibrosis' at the day-long conference, which was part of the week-long British Association Festival of Science.

Professor Hart's research represents an exciting way forward in cancer research. The number of people developing malignant melanoma in the UK is doubling every ten years. In 1986 around 3,300 people were diagnosed with melanoma and over a third of them would die from their disease.

Approval to carry out the work needs to pass one more stage before the project can begin on volunteer patients with advanced malignant melanoma. The first stage would not be an attempt at a cure but to check whether this type of gene therapy is feasible in patients.

Professor Hart explained to the conference the difficulties encountered by scientists when developing gene therapy in restricting its effects to cancer cells alone, and only activating it in the cells of their choosing.

The method the scientists have used selects the cells of their choice rather like a weedkiller on a lawn selects the weeds: the whole lawn is exposed to the weedkiller, but only the weeds are killed, the grass remaining unaffected.

Professor Hart's work centres around a piece of DNA called a promoter which controls the production of an enzyme called tyrosinase – essential for producing melanin in melanoma cells. This DNA promoter can control the switching on of genes introduced into cells.

He explained: 'We took a reporter gene, which was able to turn chemicals blue to show us the cells in which the promoter operated. We then hooked it up to the DNA promoter so the reporter gene would be switched on by the promoter once active inside a cell.'

Experiments have been carried out in tissue culture and as tumours growing in mice, but the blue colour was only seen in melanomas and types of cells which give rise to melanoma. This showed that the DNA promoter was selectively active in those cell types, providing a way of targeting, so that genes can be switched on in the tumour cells and nowhere else.

Prof. Hart explained the ways in which his team, headed by Dr Richard Vile, is hooking other genes onto the promoter to provoke an attack on the targeted tumour cells, causing them to self-destruct. Some of these genes instruct the tumour cells to produce Interleukin 2 (IL2), which stimulates the immune system to attack the cancer. They are hoping that localised production of IL2 around the tumour cells will limit side-effects in the rest of the body.

© Imperial Cancer Research Fund
September, 1994

The only hope for dying children

New advances in scientific research are the one ray of light in the lives of suffering families. Bob Wylie reports

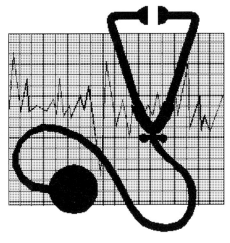

You live in hope. Day by day. Hope that they find a cure. Thus Norma O'Hagan heralded last Tuesday's publication of the first report on advances in human genetics research in Britain. For her, Britain's Human Genome Project – part of a world-wide collaboration of scientists at the frontiers of genetics – can be defined in two sentences: 'Research is the ray of light we have in our lives. If that stops what have we got?'

Norma's eight-year-old son Sean suffers from the inherited disease Duchenne Muscular Dystrophy which strikes only male children. If his life follows the common path, he will be wheelchair-bound by the time he is a teenager. Progressive muscular paralysis will distort and twist his body before claiming his life, probably before he reaches his twenties. Norma and her husband already know every single step down that path. Sean is their second son to have the disease.

Norma found out she was a carrier when her first son, Jim, was diagnosed as having the disease at Glasgow's Yorkhill Hospital when he was six. 'It was like getting hit with a brick. I cried a lot. I finished up having to do everything for him but somehow you cope with it.' When Jim died aged 16 – 10 years ago – his body was so twisted that his right hip lay over his left thigh.

The couple's second child was a girl. By the time she was pregnant with Sean, Norma could have had foetal screening tests – amniocentesis – which would have allowed her to find out if she was carrying a male and thus running a one-in-two chance of a Duchenne MD boy. But

she did not take up the offer of screening. She gambled and lost.

She did not take the screening because she knew that she could not go through with a termination. 'All I have to keep me going is that through genetics Sean will not die. I have no time for those who lecture about genetics tampering with creation. They have not experienced what I have.'

In Sean's case it will be a race against time. Techniques which may eventually allow doctors to replace the defective gene and possibly lead to a cure are still only at an early, developmental stage.

There are around 170 people with Duchenne MD in Scotland at any one time. One in every 4,500 male births in Scotland is a baby with Duchenne MD, named after the French scientist who, in 1862, first categorised the symptoms of the disease. Due to advances in understanding of genetics, doctors now know that it is caused by a defective gene in the X chromosome. This is passed to offspring by their mothers, who are carriers. The defective gene prevents production of dystrophin, a protein which is vital to muscle chemistry.

The first screening used to detect Duchenne MD was amniocentesis, developed in the early 1970s. The tests are now so advanced that doctors can tell near to 100% accuracy if the foetus is a male child who will have MD.

Heather Caldwell's family provides a neatly-packaged history of genetics and Duchenne MD rolled into one. Her mother, Babs McCallum, had two brothers who both died from MD in their twenties. At that time – the late 1950s – Babs was not even told by doctors that she could be a carrier.

Babs realised something was wrong when she recognised her first-born, Gordon, had the same strange way of walking as her brothers. She was pregnant with Heather when she found out the worst about Gordon – the first time she heard that Duchenne MD was hereditary. 'It is heartbreaking. You are watching someone dying. I can still remember the grief of watching him going out with his pals to play football and he could not kick the ball. Something as simple as that.'

The suffering Babs has endured is etched in her face. She looks older than her years. Her daughter has suffered too – watching her brother die – but genetic screening has allowed her the certainty of having a healthy daughter, Leona, without fear. Now she is expecting a second child in September, another girl.

Heather: 'I'm a 98% carrier of MD. But I've had the enormous advantage of knowledge which was denied to my mother. Everyone should be allowed to have that. To make the choice.' But would she have terminated her pregnancy if the screening had shown a male carrying Duchenne MD? 'I don't believe in abortion but I don't believe in bringing a child into the world to watch him die either. Nor would I want to put Leona through what I went through watching my brother. So I would have had to think very, very seriously.'

Anne Tudhope has not had the luxury of wondering what she would do. She had two brothers, Jim and Kenneth, who died of Duchenne MD when they were 21 and 26. When she got married to her husband Jim, they knew she was a carrier. Her first

pregnancy was identical twins. Boys. Anne knew at that time there was a 50-50 chance they would have MD. She was not willing to take the chance. 'I'd seen my brothers and I could not live with that happening to mine although it was all hugely upsetting,' she says. Now she has a family of two girls, Laura, aged 7, and Karen, 4.

Before she had Laura she and Jim were on the verge of giving up and had actually applied to adopt a child when they heard that the Medical Genetics Unit at Yorkhill could provide the screening which

could identify sex and the certainty of MD or not. The knowledge of that persuaded them to try again.

In between the girls Anne was pregnant with a boy who was identified as having MD. She had another abortion: 'It's alright for these people who decry genetics. But they don't know what Duchenne MD is. They have not lived with it.'

- Readers who wish to help genetics research can send donations to the Medical Genetics Unit at Yorkhill.

Call for public support of genetic engineering

Vital for future farming practices

A plea for a deeper understanding by the public of some of the benefits of both animal and plant genetic engineering was urged this week by Prof. Tom Blundell.

Public support for developments in agricultural science was vital if new technology was to play a central role in future farming practice, he declared.

Prof. Blundell, who is director-general of the Agricultural and Food Research Council, was giving the fourth annual lecture of the Royal Agricultural Society of England.

Great strides were being made in the bio-revolution, he said. But he understood why such developments could be accompanied by public concern.

He still believed, however, that the exciting opportunities arising from the revolutions in biology would help to satisfy the demands of consumers, environmentalists and members of the rural community.

Prof. Blundell pointed out that with genetic engineering of livestock, modern biology could identify genes for favourable traits.

This information could be used to accelerate traditional breeding approaches, particularly in pigs, cows and chickens.

By David Leach
Agricultural Editor

There were also other occasions where he felt the introduction of new genes into farm animals should be considered acceptable.

'For instance, gene technology can be used to make very expensive complex molecules in milk for the treatment of human disease such as emphysema, or to make valuable vaccines in chicken eggs.'

Prof. Blundell said new technologies could also improve the

'Ultimately it must be the public that makes the decisions about the use of biotechnology and evaluates the social, legal and economic repercussions'

quality of food, decrease the use of agrochemicals and assist diversification into other products, such as fibres, specialist chemicals, pharmaceuticals and fuel.

'They can help sustain integrated farming systems by creating wealth in the countryside and providing a greener alternative to town-based industries.'

Introducing genes from wild plants into commercial crops could possibly cut the need for agrochemicals by bolstering their resistance to various herbicides, pests and diseases.

Prof. Blundell emphasised the need to involve the public in discussions, particularly where the ethical and social implications of gene transfer were concerned.

'It is clearly the responsibility of the scientist to keep the public informed of the opportunities arising from the new biotechnologies,' he said.

'Ultimately it must be the public that makes the decisions about the use of biotechnology and evaluates the social, legal and economic repercussions.'

Pigs bred for human transplants

Transgenic pigs which could end waiting-lists for human donor organs have been reared at a secret research centre

By Laura Kibby

Transplants using pig organs could be commonplace within three years, scientists in Britain have claimed.

Litters of transgenic pigs, with a genetic make-up which will hopefully not cause humans to reject transplants, have been reared at a secret Cambridge centre.

The breakthrough could soon mean that patients will be able to receive hearts, lungs, kidneys and pancreases from specially bred pigs.

The results have been welcomed by doctors who believe that such genetic transfer may herald the end of waiting-lists for human donor organs.

John Wallwork, consultant cardiothoracic surgeon and director of the Papworth Hospital heart/lung transplant programme, said: 'The need is for many thousands of organs a year. Half of the patients waiting die before they can have operations and it would be wonderful to be able to start operating at nine in the morning and carry on transplanting knowing there is no shortage.'

The breakthrough follows the successful breeding of the second litter of transgenic pigs which could form the basis of clinical trials on humans.

Dr David White, the Cambridge University scientist at the forefront of the discovery, said: 'We can now get exactly the same response from the pigs as we would from a human being.

'The problem with this type of transplant has always been almost immediate rejection of the organ by the patient. Now, having been able to recreate human proteins in the pigs, the patient's immune system should not reject the pig's organ. We could have the first transplants within two years but realistically it would be more likely to be three years away.' Dr White speculated that there could be a tenfold increase in the number of transplants.

The breeding programme is carried out under strict security to avoid attacks by animal activists and will continue until 1995, with the possibility of clinical trials beginning the year after.

Human gene material containing the vital proteins is injected into sows' eggs. The important factor, the 'complement system', switches off the defence action that the body's cells produce when they come in contact with foreign matter.

By introducing complement into the pig, the human system is fooled into accepting the organs as human and not destroying them.

The Edinburgh biotechnology company Pharmaceutical Proteins (PPL) is one of the world's leading companies in the development of transgenic technology.

In 1990, it bred Tracy the 'superewe', Britain's first transgenic sheep, and it is now getting near the development of the world's first production flock of sheep whose milk might be used in the treatment of emphysema and possibly cystic fibrosis.

Genetically engineered chickens have also been produced at the Government-funded Animal Research Institute, in Roslin, south of Edinburgh. It is hoped the eggs could be used in the treatment of haemophilia

In 1905 a French doctor tried to transplant a pig's kidney into a man dying of renal failure. Five years later a German patient was kept alive for 30 hours after being given a monkey's kidney. The longest survival record belongs to a man who lived for nine months in 1963 after getting a chimpanzee's kidney in an operation in New Orleans.

© *The Scotsman*
March, 1995

Uses of genetically engineered animals

From the RSPCA Research Animals Department

The RSPCA is concerned both with the ethical and the welfare problems associated with genetically engineered animals. In this article the Research Animals Department summarises current uses of animals in genetic engineering and the welfare concerns that arise. The ethical problems are also very important but dealing with these in detail is not within the remit of this article.

Genetically engineered animals have been developed for a number of purposes:
- Production of pharmaceuticals;
- As farm animals with 'improved' production;
- As 'models' to study disease;
- As 'models' of human genetic disorders to develop human gene therapy.
- To change the character of animal organs to try to make them suitable for transplanting into humans.

Production of pharmaceuticals

Animals have been genetically engineered to secrete proteins for use as pharmaceuticals. Mice are used initially to test systems out. Other animals such as sheep and goats are then used for large-scale production. One example is sheep which secrete human blood-clotting protein (Factor IX), used for treating haemophiliacs, in their milk. Sheep have also been genetically engineered to secrete alpha-1 antitrypsin, used in treatment of emphysema and cystic fibrosis. Products from these animals are currently undergoing clinical trials. Both types of sheep are transgenic because they have a human gene inserted into their own chromosomes. In neither of these cases were there any reported welfare problems with the sheep.

'Improved' farm animal production

Research in this field is motivated by the desire both to increase the efficiency of food production by changing certain characteristics such as the proportion of body fat or milk yields, and to improve disease resistance. Production of transgenic farm animals is a significant area of concern to animal welfare groups for two reasons:
- Animals could be developed to tolerate intensive farming systems.
- Deleterious and unpredicted side-effects may occur. An example is the case of the Beltsville pig in the USA. The gene for human growth hormone was inserted into these animals in order to try to improve growth rates and leanness. The pigs suffered a number of adverse side-effects, including arthritis and lameness.

In cases where the intended characteristics are economically desirable, there is a risk that deleterious effects on the health and welfare of the animals will be ignored.

Laboratory models of disease/organ transplants

Animals are used in medical research as 'models' for humans, although they are obviously imperfect substitutes. Genetically engineered animals have been developed to try to improve the relevance of these disease models and there has been a tremendous increase in the number produced in recent years. The animals are predetermined to develop a particular medical condition, for example, cystic fibrosis, muscular dystrophy, cancer, sickle cell anaemia. The majority of animals used are mice.

There are obviously ethical and welfare concerns about using animals in research where animals are caused pain, suffering or distress.

It is difficult to assess whether the welfare (as opposed to the ethical) problems with genetically engineered animals are any different from those associated with the use of animals in experiments as a whole. In welfare terms, the crucial issue is whether the animals suffer, and it is debatable whether the problems are any worse if an animal is born predisposed to develop a disease as a result of genetic engineering than if such a condition is induced by standard methods.

If genetically engineered animals provide more specific disease models, then this could result in more focused research and an eventual reduction in animal use. However, there will be an escalation in animal use before this stage is reached.

In the UK, pigs have been genetically engineered with a view to using their hearts and kidneys for human transplants. There have not been any reported welfare problems with the pigs themselves however; the associated research, e.g. between animal organ transplants and development of immunosuppressant regimes, will cause animal suffering. The ethics of using animals as a source of organs for human transplants is currently being seriously debated.

There is a further way that genetic engineering is likely to impinge on animals. This is where products of genetic engineering (e.g. medical products, pesticides, novel foods) have to be assessed for safety before they can be used. The safety testing regulations are likely to involve tests on animals which can cause them pain and suffering.

*© RSPCA Research Animals Department
November, 1995*

Genetics milestone may be key to the code of life

Steve Connor reports on work that could help create a living artificial organism from scratch

Scientists working for a private company have reached a milestone in genetics by reading all the genetic secrets of a free-living organism for the first time.

The researchers have sequenced all the 1.8 million 'letters' of a microbe's DNA, raising the prospect that one day they could synthesise the same blueprint to create an artificial life-form from scratch.

Deciphering the entire genetic sequence of *Hemophilus influenzae*, a bacterium that causes infectious illnesses in humans, will also help scientists to design more effective drugs and vaccines against the disease.

Craig Venter, an American scientist from the Institute for Genomic Research in Gaithersburg, Maryland, who fell out with the US scientific establishment over the patent rights to gene sequences, made the breakthrough with funding from a private company, Human Genome Sciences.

Dr Venter presented details of the research at a closed meeting of the American Society for Microbiology earlier this week and has refused to comment further until the work is published.

According to yesterday's *New York Times*, Dr Venter had applied for public funding from the US National Institutes of Health but had been refused on the grounds that his approach would not work. Now the commercial rights to the research are owned by Human Genome Sciences.

In addition to deciphering all 1,830,121 building blocks of Hemophilus DNA, Dr Venter said his team sequenced the 580,067 chemical bases that make up the genetic blueprint of a second free-living microbe, *Mycoplasma genitalium*, one of the simplest, single-celled organisms.

John Sulston, director of the Medical Research Council's Sanger Centre at Cambridge, said the research was an 'exciting milestone' in the international effort to decode the genetic sequences of various life forms, including the human genome.

He said that although it is now theoretically possible to synthesise the same genetic blueprint in the laboratory, there were still immense problems in using such a chemical code of life to create a new man-made strain of bacteria.

'Even if it was possible to get all 1.8 million DNA bases in the right place, you don't just get life from DNA alone,' he said. Dr Sulston is sequencing the entire genome of a nematode worm.

Frederick Blattner, Professor of Genetics at Wisconsin University, said it was still not known what would happen if scientists were able to synthesise the entire blueprint of a free-living organism. 'I don't know how you'd get it jump-started.'

If scientists wanted to create a new, artificial strain of Hemophilus by making a DNA blueprint from scratch, they would have to insert the genetic material into existing cultures of the bacteria in the hope of 'transforming' them, Professor Blattner said.

One of the most important immediate benefits of the research is that more benign strains of the bacteria can be compared with more dangerous types in order to develop better drugs or vaccines against the disease, he said.

'It's a very important achievement and an incredibly important objective. It's the first time a free-standing life-form has been determined,' Professor Blattner said.

Until now the only life-forms that have been fully sequenced are viruses, which are incapable of living outside the living cells of other organisms. They have much simpler genetic blueprints because they lack basic life-support mechanisms.

Hemophilus bacteria have about 1,750 genes and, according to Dr Venter, they fall in 14 different categories that include 'all the enzymes necessary for life'.

© The Independent
May, 1995

Potential advantages and disadvantages

t is difficult to predict either benefits or adverse effects of genetic engineering. However, these may include:

Potential advantages
Genetic engineering techniques in vaccine production could lead to a reduction in use of animals for safety testing as happened with hepatitis B vaccine. It could also lead to development of better vaccines for animal diseases. For example, use of the genetically engineered oral rabies vaccine protects foxes from disease and provides an alternative to killing them as a method of disease control.

Products of genetic engineering (such as 'human' insulin for treating diabetics) could replace animals as the source of this material.

The use of genetically engineered products for diagnosing disease may reduce current animal use for this purpose.

The technique may be helpful in identifying genes responsible for disease or malformations in animals.

More relevant animal 'models' in medical research may lead to an overall reduction in animal usage.

Genetically engineered products for agricultural use may be less destructive to animals and the environment than traditionally used chemicals.

Potential disadvantages
Modifications of the genome to 'improve' farm animal production may result in unpredicted deleterious malformations. There could be significant welfare problems associated with, for example, changing the size, reproductive capacity or physiological/biochemical constitution of animals. This could result in reduced mobility, metabolic disease, difficulties in giving birth, skeletal problems. Some problems may not become apparent for several generations when the animals are not under regulatory controls.

Genetic engineering is an expanding science and the number of animals used in research (with the associated pain, suffering or distress) is increasing.

Creating transgenic animals is still rather 'hit and miss' and a very high number of animals are used in the process. Many of these animals will not express the required genetic characteristics (i.e. will not be transgenic) and their lives will have been wasted. In addition there may be unpredicted adverse effects which compromise the animals' welfare.

The manipulation of genetic material is considered to be unethical by some individuals and organisations, whatever the likely benefits may be.

© RSPCA Research Animals Department

Disadvantages of biotechnology

We asked people what, if any, they thought might be the disadvantages of biotechnology. We did not prompt them in any way.

Moral and ethical issues and product safety are seen as disadvantages by the largest groups of people (18% and 17% respectively).

The most frequent 'other' replies concerned unwanted side-effects and concern that biotechnology was 'meddling' with nature.

Overall, however, fewer people mentioned disadvantages than had previously mentioned advantages, although only 10% of respondents said that they did not believe that there were disadvantages. The largest single group of people, however, was those who 'don't know' what the disadvantages might be.

● The above is an extract from *Consumers and Biotechnology*, a report conducted for the Food and Drink Federation. See page 39 for address details.

© The Food and Drink Federation
September, 1995

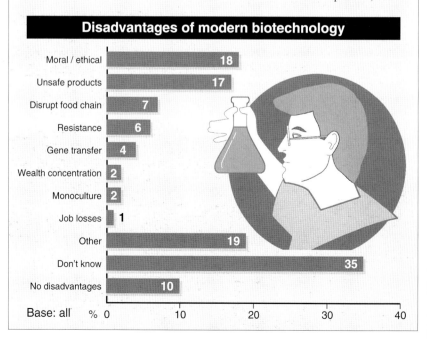

Disadvantages of modern biotechnology

	%
Moral / ethical	18
Unsafe products	17
Disrupt food chain	7
Resistance	6
Gene transfer	4
Wealth concentration	2
Monoculture	2
Job losses	1
Other	19
Don't know	35
No disadvantages	10

Base: all   %   0   10   20   30   40

Biotechnology report

Based on research conducted for the Food and Drink Federation

foodfuture

- 68% of the population know nothing at all about biotechnology or have never heard of it. This figure is echoed by a later finding that 64% of the population have received no information at all about biotechnology.

- Only 6% of the general public claim to know 'a great deal' or a 'fair amount' about biotechnology. Those who claim to be better informed are more likely to: claim to be very interested in new developments in science and technology; have finished education aged 19 or more; be in the AB social group; be male.

- Respondents who claim to be better informed about biotechnology are more likely than average to see the benefits of biotechnology and to identify groups who might benefit from it.

- Nearly half of all respondents (46%) see some benefit connected with food and 30% see benefits in the medical field

- Farmers/growers are the group thought by most people to be likely to benefit from biotechnology, with food manufacturers the next group mentioned. People are much more likely to see benefits for other groups than for themselves and their families.

- When asked which groups might benefit most, developing countries and farmers/growers were mentioned equally.

- Fewer people identified disadvantages than benefits of biotechnology. Only 10% of people, however, saw no disadvantages, with more than one-third saying that they didn't know. Moral/ethical disadvantages and unsafe products were mentioned by the largest groups of people (18% and 17% respectively).

- The majority of people (53%) support continuing development of modern biotechnology for disease resistance in animals. Apart from this, however, people are more likely to support development for plant applications rather than animal applications.

- Those who are better informed about biotechnology are more likely to support continuing development across a range of applications.

- Only 2% of respondents are very confident that the controls surrounding the applications of biotechnology in food and agriculture are adequate, with a further quarter (27%) fairly confident. More than two-thirds of adults, therefore, have little or no confidence or are unsure.

The above is an extract from *Consumers and biotechnology*, a report on research conducted for the Food and Drink Federation. See page 39 for address details.

Four legs very good

This week Imutran, a bio-tech company, said it had successfully transplanted pig hearts into monkeys, a step towards use in humans. Transplant pioneer Terence English points to the problems; opposite, a Muslim and an opponent of vivisection give their views

In the light of the recent announcement made by Imutran that genetically engineered pig hearts have been transplanted into monkeys with encouraging results of short-term survival, we ought to consider the ethical and scientific problems in transplanting animal organs into humans.

Although successful heart transplants were performed during the 1970s – through the use of immuno-suppression with steroids and azathioprine – it was not until the new drug cyclosporine became available in the early 1980s that large numbers of heart transplants began to be undertaken worldwide. Control of the rejection process which follows the transplantation of any tissue grew more predictable; costs were reduced, and expectation of survival after heart transplants improved. Soon, the number of heart transplants was limited mostly by the availability of donor hearts.

So it was reasonable that those involved in the field should have turned their attention to alternative substitutes for heart replacement. The most obvious were mechanical devices or animal organs. An enormous amount of time and money has been spent on developing mechanical heart substitutes. Although the fist pneumatically driven total artificial heart was inserted in 1984, problems with the bio-compatibility of the lining of the blood pump, and with the design of a reliable implantable power source, have meant that current devices remain imperfect.

And although recently there has been renewed interest in the implantation of 'ventricular assist devices', acting in parallel with the failing heart which is left in place, we still seem to be some years away from a reliable, cheap, totally implantable mechanical device that will take over the action of the human heart.

It is not surprising that in the last few years there has been intense interest in the possible application of 'xenotransplantation' – transplanting tissue or organs across species. In this situation the tendency to rejection is much more vigorous and difficult to control than when transplanting within species.

Pig valves have been used for many years to help patients as a replacement for their diseased human valves

When thinking of using animal organs for transplanting into man, there are two main problems: scientific/immunological, and ethical.

The object of the Cambridge Group, as represented by Imutran, has been to breed a herd of pigs so genetically engineered that the immunological reaction of a primate to pig antigens is much diminished. Their recent experiments suggest that they have considerably ameliorated the monkey's early reaction to reject a pig heart. At this stage doubt must remain over the likelihood of long-term successful immuno-suppression of a pig heart in a human. Yet the encouraging results now reported in monkeys make it much more likely that the experiment will be attempted. We need to ask if there are ethical reasons why animal organs should *not* be used in humans. In the mid-1980s, there was an outcry in the US when a surgeon in California transplanted a baboon heart into a new-born baby with severe heart disease, and the child died 28 days later.

Many people, though, would be sympathetic to using pigs rather than primates for this purpose. Pigs are bred in large numbers for eating. And pig valves have been used for many years to help patients as a replacement for their diseased human valves. Indeed, only earlier this week I inserted a pig valve into a patient. Should a big ethical distinction be drawn between using the valves from pig hearts and using the whole heart?

Many of us of would feel not. My own belief is that the larger ethical problem is one for the individual surgical team involved in the experiments so far – they will know whether or not they have arrived at a level of understanding and control of the profound immunological reaction which will let them proceed responsibly, and with confidence, to the stage of human experimentation.

● Sir Terence English is consultant cardiac surgeon at Papworth Hospital, Cambridge, and President of the British Medical Association. He performed the UK's first successful heart transplant in 1979.

Zaki Badawi explains the Islamic position

The Koran decrees in four different verses that Muslims are not permitted to eat the flesh of pigs. Some schools of law reasoned that this ruling is because the pig is an unclean animal; if you touch a pig with a wet hand, you will have to wash your hand seven times, using in one wash dust mixed with water as a form of cleanser.

It might be assumed that such an unclean animal would be unsuitable for organ transplants to Muslims. But this is not so. Indeed, the genetic engineers' success is welcome news.

Why? First and foremost, the Koran prohibits the *eating* of the pig. Other uses can be assumed to be permitted. Indeed, some of the schools of law consider all living animals, including the pig, to be ritually clean, and permit the use of its leather and hair, even for toothbrushes.

Secondly, one of the principal aims of Islamic law (*sharia*) is the preservation of life. All means are permissible to achieve this. Under the law of necessity, the scholars permit a Muslim to eat pig flesh to keep alive if there is no alternative food. They go further, to say that if life depends on consuming the pig, it becomes an obligation upon a Muslim to do so.

Clearly, a transplant is to save a life, and is permissible under all schools of law. When the organ becomes part of a human body, it at once acquires human dignity and value. Those concerned with animal rights might object: but people breed animals to eat, and it would illogical to object to breeding for transplants. It might also be objected that introducing human genes into these pigs has made them semi-human, and so inviolable. This is hardly acceptable: pigs remain pigs. Characteristics arising from genetic engineering do not transform them into humans.

There remains the more serious question of the moral limits of human engineering. To the layman like myself, the geneticists are acquiring such powers as to be almost god-like. There is fear they may use their skill to determine the future of the human species and even embark upon a project of creating a master race of superhumans.

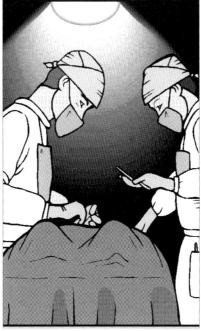

If such a power is conceivable, then the activities of the scientists must be regulated. We must protect our species from becoming factory-produced, and programmed by a few powerful scientists. It is bad enough to suffer the control of our minds by the modern media; we don't want to be completely programmed by the scientists.

● Zaki Badawi is Principal of the Muslim College, London, and Chairman of the Sharia Council.

This will now force us to consider what it means to be human, says Malcolm Eames

This is just one of the many new genetic technologies which may revolutionise healthcare. Before succumbing to technological entrancement, I would suggest five questions society should address.

Will it work?
Amidst the hype and the hope, remember that this announcement was not a first. Similar experiments have been reported in the US, with survival times between four and 30 hours. Even if these figures have been improved upon, Imutran's research clearly remains extremely preliminary. If the immediate problems of 'hyperacute' rejection are overcome, many fundamental biological barriers remain. In the short to medium term, the technique is unlikely to improve transplant availability.

It is safe?
In the US, there has been concerned debate over the possible dangers of disease transmission. Although generally considered to be more remote in the case of pigs, the risk of some new pathogen crossing the species barrier must be considered. To minimise this, animals will be carefully screened and maintained in sterile environments. But the dangers are real and cannot be ignored.

What are the alternatives?
Much could be done to improve the current situation. Preventative healthcare and changes to donor recruitment policy have enormous potential to alleviate shortages of organs, and represent a far more intelligent and humane approach.

Is it acceptable?
It is suggested that while most of us eat meat, the ethical acceptability of using animal organs for medical purposes should be beyond dispute. But the question here is whether it is right to engineer animals genetically for human ends. The public is not convinced: a recent Eurobarometer poll suggested that only 14 per cent of the European public would support the use of genetic engineering to develop lifesaving drugs where animal suffering was involved. We most also ask at what point is the species barrier crossed, and exactly how much human genetic material must these pigs contain before they are accorded those rights currently reserved for humans.

Where do we draw the line?
It is certain that as science gives us new opportunities to exploit animals, it will also force us to consider what it is to be human. Genetic engineering will change our relationship with animals. It will pose more ethical choices – which will determine the kind of world we live in and what kind of (genetic) animals we will become.

● Dr Malcolm Eames is on the board of the Genetics Forum and Head of Information and Research for the British Union for the Abolition of Vivisection. © *The Guardian August, 1995*

Ethics of heartless pigs

Letters to the editor

Your article (*Four legs very good*, August 25) is a welcome contribution to the public discussion about using animal organs for transplantation into humans. In January, the Nuffield Council on Bioethics established a working party under the chairmanship of Professor Albert Weale to report on relevant ethical issues.

The working party has consulted extensively and the Council expects to be able to publish the report this winter. For once this report will provide for a wide-ranging discussion before the application of a new biomedical technology.

The Council disagrees with Sir Terence English's belief 'that the larger ethical problem is one for the individual surgical team involved in the experiments so far'.

Quite apart from the issues raised by Dr Eames of the British Union for the Abolition of Vivisection, thought must be given to the likely costs of xenografts. These costs will be high and will raise questions of opportunity costs for the National Health Service.

There are great uncertainties about this new technique. Should we not set up in advance a system for monitoring and, if necessary, regulating these procedures? Early recipients of xenografts must be studied carefully and their quality of life will need to be assessed, preferably by those not involved in the surgical team.

This should indicate the wide range of issues to be tackled before the introduction of xenografts into practice.

David Shapiro
Executive Secretary,
Nuffield Council
on Bioethics
28 Bedford Square,
London
WC1B 3EG

Dr Malcom Eames frames the key philosophical issues of xenotransplantation nicely. The suggestion that this technology 'will now force us to consider what it means to be human', however, is misguided. 'Human' is a word which, when properly employed, references the species, homo sapiens, any individual of that class, or (as an adjective) anything representative of that class (e.g. human language, human habitats).

While there are genetic criteria used for establishing what gets included in the set 'things human', the principle criterion employed by evolutionary biologists is the ability of individuals of that set to interbreed. Thus, a doe-eyed individual with chicken's lips and a pig's heart would still be rightly counted as a 'human', so long as the individual has not become reproductively isolated from his conspecifics as a result of the procedure which endowed him with those characteristics.

Whether a chicken-lipped man would find himself reproductively isolated when prospective mates learn that he is a pig at heart is another matter. We do not wonder if an individual with a pacemaker or of with a prosthesis is less human and more machine. The important category for morals and law – i.e. for the rational basis of our treatment of one another, and of our differential solicitude towards other species – will remain personhood.

J Ellis Perry IV
j.e.perry@abdn.ac.uk

The fewer pigs (and other animals) that we eat, the less likely we are to develop heart disease, and the less likely we are to need these ghoulish animals for human transplants. If John Wallwork of Imutran were honestly 'in the business of making lives better', why not work on preventive methods? After all, heart disease is one of the most avoidable conditions around. I expect it's probably less profitable.

Joseph Ryan
76 Northumberland Road,
Manchester M16 9PP

Instead of this obsessive searching for grotesque ways to prolong life, why do we not devote what little is left of our wisdom to studying the acceptance of death? It would make things much easier for all of us, whether we happen to be a human, a chimpanzee or a pig.

Alison Prince
Burnfoot
Whiting Bay,
Isle of Arran
KA27 8QL

Engineering answers to question of genes

Genetic frontiers are extended week by week. Bob Wylie examines the moral maze

Every week seems to bring news of another breakthrough in genetic science. Why?

Genetics is bound by the laws of evolution of all science – long periods of accumulation of knowledge followed by significant leaps forward.

The start of the Human Genome Project – a world-wide charter to encourage international collaboration among scientists at the forefront of genetic research – has greatly helped this. The HGP is funded with $3bn from governments, research bodies and private companies for the next 15 years.

Is Scotland contributing?

Scottish researchers are among world leaders in the race to discover the gene linked to hereditary breast cancer and have already contributed to notable breakthroughs in cystic fibrosis, muscular dystrophy and bone marrow disease.

Back to basics – what are genes and what is gene therapy?

Genes are the hereditary material in the body that determine what a living thing will be, and are passed down from one generation to the next. Defective genes can also be inherited, hence hereditary disease.

Genes are contained in DNA, or deoxyribonucleic acid, whose discovery was followed by the start of genetic engineering – isolation of genes and their identification with specific diseases. Science has since developed further to allow alteration of defective genes – gene therapy.

Gene therapy can alter the progress of disease in an individual, such as the bone marrow operation carried out on baby Carly Todd, from Glasgow, last year to change potentially fatal genetic deficiencies. But that does not affect the genetic code handed on to the next generation.

Germ line therapy can. This is the alteration of the genes in the sperm or eggs. So far as is known, this has been practised only on animals: mice have been bred with cystic fibrosis as a result of germ line therapy introducing the human CF gene. And there are pigs which have near-copies of human hearts.

Human germ line therapy is illegal, although there are suspicions it has been used in China to limit haemophilia, a genetic blood disorder.

Opponents of genetic manipulation say such developments are the thin end of a wedge tampering with evolution which will end in mutant disasters.

What then are the benefits to humanity of genetics and gene therapy?

Take cystic fibrosis, the crippling lung disease. The CF gene has now been identified. Genetic screening allows testing of parents to gauge whether they are likely to pass it on to their offspring. It also allows detection of the gene in the foetus, so affected foetuses can be aborted. The incidence of Down's syndrome and spina bifida can also be reduced in this way.

But doesn't that raise a whole range of moral controversies?

Yes. Most genetic technology involves the identification of damaged genes and the offer of therapeutic abortion to parents whose foetus is found to be affected. Specialists insist that they are only providing the right to choose.

Do those whose offspring carry a high risk of heritable disease really want to know about it?

Again this is a matter of belief. It also has to do with the nature of specific diseases. Only a minority of potential sufferers from Huntington's Chorea, for example, have taken advantage of the genetic screening available to them.

What about the spectre of creating the so-called Master Race free of any defects?

Geneticists say talk of mass sterilisations and elimination of certain groups – homosexuality may have a genetic component – which is the dangerous extreme of their science, is off the wall. The creation of a blond, blue-eyed Master Race is a genetic impossibility, they claim. Each of us carries at least 40 defective genes which in the wrong circumstances can produce defective progeny.

Does that mean there is nothing to be concerned about?

Not exactly. In America, sections of the insurance industry are already insisting that prospective clients submit to limited gene screening.

And 'designer' babies?

Sex selection by gene manipulation is illegal, but the evidence seems to show that it is now following the social rules of abortion – banned or not, the rich can always pay.

© *Scotland on Sunday*
February, 1995

The moral maze

One of Britain's most respected spiritual leaders asks whether genetic engineering is advancing too fast for society's good

Hardly a day goes by without another news story about some great scientific advance in the field of genetic engineering.

Only yesterday, we read about the genetic discovery that could extend the lifespan of human cells by up to 30 per cent – the elixir of youth that scientists have been searching for since the dawn of alchemy.

Last week, a team of researchers in the US claimed to have located the gene which causes dyslexia.

In July, British scientists claimed to have found the gene responsible for one of the diseases leading to kidney failure.

In September, Oxford scientists discovered two genes which could contribute to childhood diabetes. And last month, American and British researchers tracked down a gene responsible for a form of inherited breast cancer.

Meanwhile, there were accounts last year from the US National Cancer Institute about a genetic predisposition towards homosexuality, with the apparent discovery of the gene concerned. This led to the former Chief Rabbi, Lord Jakobovits, suggesting that, if it were possible to genetically engineer that gene out of future children, parents might choose to do so.

Suffering

The furore caused by that view was considerable: the reaction from the gay community was hostile and cries of 'eugenics' were heard throughout the land. But if we were to follow that position to its conclusion, we would have to ask whether we should be able to engineer the dyslexia gene, for instance, to stop our children suffering considerable problems?

Or whether we should be able to know that the child carried in the womb is likely to be alcoholic,

By Julia Neuberger

diabetic or have kidney failure later in life? And, if we know it, what should we do about it?

Should we be aborting such children as 'undesirable', or to prevent them suffering? Should we even want to know what the future holds for ourselves or our children?

Does it really help to have all this knowledge about our future illnesses, or is this merely too much knowledge which will make the life choices we all have to decide even harder?

For if we know we are bearing a child with a defect, we may have to decide between abortion or, where possible, treating the foetus in a dish by manipulating the gene and replacing it in the womb.

Yet perhaps the truth is that we should be leaving well alone. In the

twenties, compulsory sterilisation of mentally ill and handicapped people seemed perfectly acceptable in the US, and Marie Stopes was concerned to limit the breeding of the very poor.

Target

There was undoubtedly a sense that it was right to create the perfect human beings – in one's own image – and to limit the breeding of others.

It was only the Nazis' appalling destruction of people with learning difficulties, the mentally ill, Jews, gypsies and homosexuals that made people think again about the wisdom of eugenics.

Yet genetic engineering implies eugenics, of a sophisticated kind. If we can remove or repair one gene, we might be able to prevent cystic fibrosis, for instance, a heart-rending condition leading to early death.

We might even be able to do something about the genetic element in inherited breast cancer.

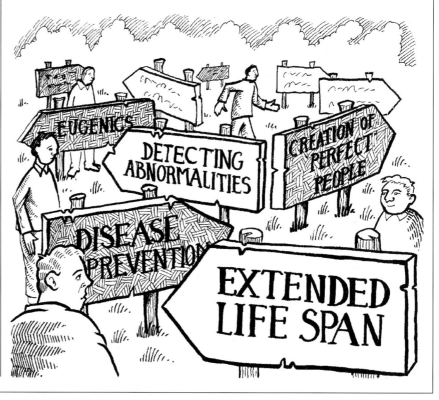

For until now it was merely thought that women with mothers and sisters who had the disease were more likely to get it, so that those seen as being at high risk, genetically speaking, occasionally had preventive double mastectomies. If it were possible to pinpoint more accurately those women at risk, we might be able to target them better and treat them preventively.

We are not there yet, but the gradual ability to screen, and increasingly to engineer, genetically makes such possibilities more likely.

Few people would quarrel with doing something for people with cystic fibrosis. Still fewer would quarrel with doing something to halt the relentlessly growing death-rate from breast cancer of women in the UK and world-wide. But even so, the ethical issues won't go away.

First among these is the question of creating 'perfect' human beings. Some of our talent may well be genetically transmitted – such as our degree of musicality, for instance, or our mathematical ability – as well as some of our defects.

A world a century hence when genetically transmitted diseases have been virtually eliminated might see the genetic engineers' attention turning to creating geniuses of one sort or other. There are already sperm banks in the US which sell the seed of Nobel prize-winners to ambitious would-be mothers, so such a picture is not entirely unrealistic.

Value

We should be terribly uneasy about this. The use of genetic engineering to provide healing for terrible diseases is one thing, morally speaking, although even that requires strict legal and ethical governance – and full consent and the maintenance of confidentiality would be essential.

But the creation of super-children is quite different, and begs many questions, including what value is put on those of us who are less than perfect. Does it suggest we should have been treated genetically, or discarded?

We must take care to regulate genetic engineering, and particularly gene therapy, in humans. Gene therapy is now vetted after the

Polkinghorne Committee considered it in depth.

But even if regulations are strict in the UK, other countries will not be so demanding. Gene therapy is where abuse could take place, and also where public understanding has not yet caught up with the speed of scientific advance.

There are already sperm banks in the US which sell the seed of Nobel prize-winners to ambitious would-be mothers

---

For the eugenicists may be in the ascendant in some countries where the birth-rate is too high, where parents are only allowed to produce one child, where infertility treatments are growing and where the prospect of the perfect child seems remarkably attractive. Strict controls are necessary, with some international force. But so is a public debate about what is acceptable, nationally and internationally.

Urgent

In genetic screening, however, there is the beginning of a genuine public debate, as a result of the work of the Nuffield Council on Bioethics and its report published late last year.

Should insurance companies be able to require genetic screening when it would materially affect policies? How should society deal with confidentiality? Should screening ever be required by employers, so that they know everything they can about us? These are some of the questions with which we have to grapple.

But there is an urgent need for public debate, so that people can decide which kinds of interventions are acceptable, and which are not, what we should try to prevent, and what we should not, and who, ultimately, should take control of this fascinating, but deeply disturbing, series of scientific advances.

● Julia Neuberger is a rabbi and a member of the Human Fertilisation and Embryology Authority.

*© Daily Mail
October, 1995*

21

Transgenic pigs

**The moral implications of animal transplants will disturb many.
But an eminent Cambridge don says we should rejoice.**

By Dr Terence Kealey

The revelation that scientists at Cambridge University have successfully transplanted the hearts from genetically altered pigs into monkeys is the most wonderful news to have emerged from the world of medicine for more than a decade. We are all too familiar with the bad side of science – here is a cause for rejoicing. The implications are stunning. We are witnessing the beginning of a major step forward in human happiness. And, wonderfully, it is British.

The chance now exists that hundreds of thousands of people who are waiting for heart, liver and kidney transplants, and would die because of the lack of donors, will now live. Sufferers from many other diseases also face hope.

Put simply, what the scientists from Imutran, the company responsible for the research, have done is to find a way to trick the human immune system of the primate, like us and monkeys, into accepting an organ from a pig. Until now we could not transplant animal organs because no pharmacologist could prevent our immune system from rejecting them. For several years scientists have been able to take an egg from the ovary of a pig, inject human genes into it, fertilise it and put it back into the sow for it to grow quite normally.

What is new is that scientists have now been able to make this pig egg appear human to our immune system, so that it can be transplanted without rejection.

Every human being is unique. In most respects, including the philosophical ones, that is desirable. But for the transplant surgeon it has been a nightmare.

The uniqueness of individual cells is crucial to normal survival. The immune system is like a policeman. It regularly monitors every cell.

If it recognises a cell as safe then it moves on. But if it encounters something alien it pounces, killing with ruthless dispatch. For most of the time the immune system kills millions of bacteria and viruses, because these are recognised as being foreign and without that inbuilt immune surveillance all of us would die in days. As everybody knows, the transplant of hearts, livers and kidneys to other humans has become almost routine. Although rejection remains a problem with many patients, it is no longer the limiting factor for transplantation. That remains the shortage of potential donors.

Put crudely, not enough healthy people are killed in accidents and so hundreds of thousands of patients die every year, across the globe, for the lack of suitable donor organs.

This is why this week's announcement is so spectacular.

Not only will all those who need these major organ transplants be treated, but whole new therapies will emerge. Many cancers, for example, are now treated by chemotherapy or radiotherapy, but in future it might be kinder, safer and more effective to just transplant the affected organ.

Other patients suffer from inherited metabolic defects such as the porphyria which afflicted King George III. A cure in the future will be a liver transplant.

Diabetes might be treated with a pancreas transplant. Psoriasis might be treated with a skin cell transplant. Cystic fibrosis might be treated with multiple organ transplants.

Possibilities are nearly endless and truly amazing. A whole new era of health and longevity is now dawning.

Of course, some organs are not transplantable. The brain, for example, is not a potential donor organ – though parts of it might be transplanted to treat Parkinson's disease. The pig is the animal of choice for most transplant operations as it most resembles the human, but one day other animal organs, too, will be available.

Philosophers may worry that some aspects of humanness might be adulterated by the use of animal organs. But heart, liver and the like have never been identified as the seat of the soul or the intellect.

What is becoming increasingly clear is that these organs are solely mechanical and will not be regarded as exclusive to us. I anticipate, therefore, no ethical objections to this treatment. If we kill pigs for food, then why should we not kill them for life saving?

I must admit, however, that there may be something distasteful in actually eating a slightly humanised pig, although it will not look like one; and I must admit also that it might one day be theoretically possible to transplant the human brain into a pig – despite ethical objections – but these are matters that will need to be decided by society over the next few decades.

We have, of course, some time to go before this experimental programme, which has been restricted to monkeys, becomes routine for humans, but we can predict with complete certainty that it will eventually be possible to customise pigs.

Initially, humans will have to accept 'off-the-peg' organs, from animals which will have been doctored to have organs reasonably similar to those of large groups of people.

But, in the near future, it will be possible to generate families of pigs individually tailored for every single one of us. Then we will have organs and blood readily available in case of emergencies.

In 100 years' time, it may well be routine for godparents to present each child with his or her own pig family, specially bred on a scientific farm.

The role of British scientists should not be underplayed. The structure and function of DNA were discovered in London and Cambridge during the early 1950s, and it is very appropriate that this clinical application of DNA should also be taking place in Cambridge.

But, of course, research continues world-wide and the Human Gerome Project, which is largely funded by America, promises the eradication of almost all inherited human diseases and undesirable traits.

Pigs will be tailored for each of us so we have organs for emergencies. Godparents may give children their own pigs, bred on a scientific farm

---

The only disadvantage I can anticipate is the intrusion of busybodies and self-appointed ethical experts who will, as ever, seek to restrict human happiness to maximise their power over the rest of us.

We quiver on the brink of a wonderful revolution in medicine, and the dynamics of our advances in biochemistry, molecular biology, immunology and surgery will shower happiness and relief on generations to come.

● Dr Terence Kealey is a university lecturer and consultant in clinical biochemistry at Addenbrooke's Hospital, Cambridge.

© The Daily Mail
September, 1995

Animal welfare implications of genetic engineering

Genetic engineering involves changing the genetic material (i.e. the genes[1]) of living organisms. The technique can be applied to viruses, bacteria, plants and animals. The genetic material of individual organisms within species can be modified, or genetic material may be transferred between species or between organisms. In the latter case a transgenic organism results.

(NB: Traditional breeding involves manipulating genetic material but by selection of specific characteristics within a single species and at the 'whole animal' level. This may also give rise to serious welfare problems.)

Genetic engineering is a complex subject encompassing many different scientific disciplines in industry, agriculture, veterinary medicine and human medicine. It is a rapidly developing technology which may have both advantages and disadvantages for human and animal health and welfare, for the environment, and in socio-economic terms.

Concern over genetic engineering arises from:
● Ethical/religious concerns relating to the manipulation of genetic material ('playing God');
● The increasing use of animals in this research field, and the predictable and unpredictable adverse effects of such research on animal welfare;
● Concern over the effects of genetically engineered products on human and animal welfare;
● Fear of the effects of genetically modified organisms, plants or animals on the environment.

[1] Genes form part of the basic structure of all living organisms. They are the 'building blocks' of chromosomes which occur in all cells. A gene contains hereditary information and so determines the characteristics of living things, for example the colour of hair or eyes.

© RSPCA – Research Animals Department

Why worry about genetic engineering?

From the Genetics Forum

Growth hormone

rBST (recombinant bovine somatotropin) is injected into cows to boost milk yields by up to 15%. Currently in use in the United States, it is used to boost productivity without regard for the animal's natural limits or tolerances and can result in gross physical distortion, stress and increased susceptibility to disease. Such non-therapeutic use of genetically engineered substances blurs the distinction between veterinary medicine and exploitation. At a time of European milk surpluses, do we really need something like rBST to 'solve' the illusory problem of milk production, given the risks to animal welfare? In addition there are still concerns over human health aspects of consuming milk from treated herds. Although use of this product is banned in the 15 European Union states until the end of 1999, the manufacturers (Eli Lilly in Merseyside and Monsanto in Austria) are lobbying to have the ban overturned. Equivalent hormonal growth promoters are being developed for pigs, sheep and fish.

Herbicide-resistant crops

Genetic engineers claim that re-engineered crops will help solve the Third World's food problems by boosting yields and reducing the need for expensive chemical inputs such as fertilisers, herbicides and pesticides. Why then are most major chemical companies investing in the development of herbicide-resistant crops which will incorporate resistance to a specific herbicide, usually one that they manufacture, thus encouraging its greater use? Far from reducing our dependence upon chemicals, increased use of herbicides is built into the manufacturer's product-development strategy.

A major concern of environmentalists is whether these new resistance traits could transfer to wild plant species via cross-pollination, producing new varieties of resistant weeds. There is evidence that this can occur, thus undermining the whole premise on which the product is based.

Pest and disease-resistant crops

Around 30% of all genetically modified crops and trees are engineered for pest and disease resistance using toxins derived from naturally occurring bio-pesticides. At present these are used selectively and intermittently by organic farmers. Intensive and widespread use might produce strong pressure for the evolution of super-pests, resistant to the most commonly used of these bio-pesticides. The introduction of toxins from non-native species such as the scorpion experiments in Oxford designed to kill cabbage caterpillars with viruses raises further questions about long-term effects on the ecosystems, when little is known about the evolution and interactive behaviour of viruses.

Genetic pollution

Once new genetically modified organisms have been released into the environment, it is not possible to recall them. The prediction of the long-term environmental consequences of such releases is a highly imprecise exercise. Regulations designed to examine these matters are limited in their scope and risk assessments exclude study of many secondary and indirect consequences. It is arguable that there should be a presumption against introducing any genetic material which could not have appeared in the ecosystem through natural mechanisms as constituting genetic pollution.

Antibiotic resistance

Some engineered crops also contain genes coding for resistance to specific antibiotics so that the success or otherwise of the modification can be tested by applying the antibiotic to destroy those plants not carrying the marker. One such, kanomycin, is in use as a last reserve drug in treating TB which is on the increase. Inappropriate encouragement of resistance to this drug could put lives at risk.

Patenting of life-forms

John Moore knows what it's like to be patented. He had his spleen removed after a diagnosis of leukaemia. When he returned for post-operative checks, his physician, Dr Golde, asked him to sign a document waiving legal rights over the removed tissue. The doctor, unbeknown to Mr Moore, had discovered that the spleen contained unusual and commercially profitable properties. He had applied to patent a cell-line derived from the spleen and had sold the research and development rights to other institutions. Mr Moore asked the California Supreme Court for a ruling on who owned 'his' genetic material. The court ruled against him – what John Moore describes as his 'essence' is now the intellectual property of someone else.

The race to control and commercialise the world's genetic resources, described as the 'enclosure of the last great commons', involves an international lobbying effort by the biotechnology industry to 'harmonise' the world's patent laws. They wish to see intellectual property law redefined to classify genetic material, whether human, animal or plant, as patentable. This would put the basic building blocks of life on the same commercial footing as a photocopying machine There are presently no clear legal mechanisms for applying any moral or ethical test before granting patent applications, nor is there any channel for society to say where the limits should be set. Patents on animals are set to proliferate. Harvard University, with the backing of Dupont Chemicals, are seeking to patent a new strain of genetically engineered mouse, the Onco-mouse, which will as it matures automatically develop cancer. The patent has been granted in the United States and is provisionally valid in Europe but is being contested by animal welfare groups.

Gene piracy

The Neem tree is found in most backyards all over India. For centuries local people have known about the tree's anti-pesticidal, anti-infective properties and have used it to keep away malaria-carrying mosquitoes, to protect stored grain from weevil and as a skin treatment. Now a number of large chemical companies have patented the tree's beneficial genes as a basis for new skin creams, bio-pesticides and even toothpaste! So now every useful aspect of the tree, known and freely available to local people, is being commercialised by US companies claiming they 'discovered these useful characteristics' – which is a bit like Columbus claiming to have discovered America!

Genetic testing in humans.

You can now test for cystic fibrosis using a kit purchased from a mail-order company. This is an incurable disease. What counselling would you need before you decide to take the test and what would you need afterwards to help you live with the knowledge that you're carrying a gene for this condition. What obligations do you have to tell your future spouse or your brothers and sisters? Does your employer or insurance company have the right to insist that you share this knowledge?

Genetic screening

Such screening of groups of individuals for suspected heritable disease or disability presupposes that the information will permit some useful choices to be made. There is as yet

no regulation or ban on employers, insurance companies or even governments undertaking such screening or using the findings for their own purposes irrespective of the well-being of the individual. People who are HIV positive know all about the effects of screening – they can be discriminated against when applying for credit, mortgages, public services or insurance cover.

Gene therapy

Soon, we'll have the technology to correct deficiencies in our genetic make-up so that we don't pass them on to our offspring. We may need cures for disease and for life-threatening disabilities, but do we need to correct every defect and blemish? Who will decide what is a legitimate use of gene therapy, who will regulate the technology to ensure that a commercial market in 'designer' genes does not develop?

Gene food

We now have the means to transfer genes between unrelated species to produce 'transgenic foods'. For, example, it's possible to insert the gene of a fish (the arctic flounder) into a tomato plant to produce a variety which can withstand freezing temperatures. This ability to transfer animal genes into plants raises a whole set of ethical, religious and cultural problems. Genes from an animal source will be unacceptable to vegetarians, just as genes from pigs and cattle will not be acceptable to Muslims, Jews and Hindus. How will we know that genetically engineered foods do not violate our ethical and religious beliefs? Current proposals for labelling gene foods do not resolve all the possible troublesome permutations.

Biodiversity

In an age when we are all becoming aware of the need to protect the diversity of life on our planet and to practice sustainable use of our natural heritage, genetic engineering may, despite claims to the contrary, be leading us down the opposite track. The promotion of crop super-strains, the elimination of natural variation, the emphasis on nature as a production tool to be fine-tuned to produce more for us to consume – all run counter to the direction that responsible environmentalists believe we should take.

© The Genetics Forum
September, 1995

Ethical implications of transgenic animal production

From Compassion In World Farming (CIWF)

By Dr Tim O'Brien

The practice of gene transfer can have considerable negative effects on farm animal welfare, from the treatment of the 'parent' animals, right through the lives of the transgenic progeny, and potentially through into successive generations.

The social and behavioural needs of the donor and recipient animals are frequently disregarded – for example, the pigs which are being used to produce organs for xeno-transplants in America have been filmed being held indoors, in pens with concrete floors, under artificial lights. Their progeny are very likely to be confined to similar inert conditions. The pig is a highly intelligent and social animal – its natural home is in a family group, close to or within woodland, where it grubs around in the soil with its fellows.

The bodies of the donor, intermediate and surrogate animals are often violated (superovulation, artificial insemination, oviduct flushing, embryo implantation), with no benefit whatsoever to the animal.

Genes from another species are implanted into recipient animals, all too frequently with damaging effect on the physiological balance of the target animal.

The idea has been suggested of using transgenic techniques to create animals which are habituated to factory-farming conditions. Compassion In World Farming maintains that, just as it is unacceptable to imprison farm animals in intensive systems such as the battery cage or veal crate, it is completely unacceptable to subject animals to pain and suffering in order to create transgenic hybrids which are capable of enduring the suffering which factory-farming inevitably inflicts.

If we allow the genetic engineering of farm animals to go ahead, we are opening up a whole new era in humanity's exploitation of animals, in which morality will take second place to expediency.

The focus of transgenic research has shifted radically in recent years. It has moved from being a science, to being a technology, serving the farming 'industry', and associated multinational companies. The highly competitive nature of the industry is hardly conducive to an ethical approach. The public's view on the matter, though, is very clear:

A recent opinion poll carried out on behalf of the European Commission found that only 14% of the European public would support genetic engineering where animal suffering was involved, even to develop life-saving drugs. The same survey found that animal welfare organisations are trusted by almost twice as many people to tell the truth about genetic engineering as public authorities are, and are trusted by more than five times as many people as industry on this.

Compassion In World Farming is campaigning for a complete ban on the production of transgenic farm animals. We also seek a ban on the use of farm animals for production of any other transgenic species, and we are opposed to the non-therapeutic treatment of farm animals with genetically-engineered substances.

Dr Tim O'Brien is Head of Communications and Research.

● The above is a factsheet produced by Compassion In World Farming. See page 39 for address details.

© CIWF
September, 1995

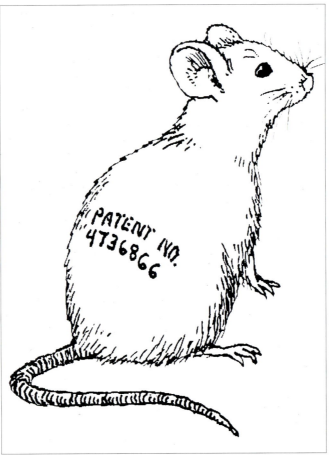

Facing up to gene genies of tomorrow

Tessa Thomas debates medical ethics with a new generation of science students

A pregnant woman goes for a routine scan at the hospital. To her horror, she is told that her baby will suffer from a condition that will stunt its growth. But, she is advised, a genetic technique may soon be available to rectify the condition. Should she keep the baby? Should she one day volunteer it for 'experimental' gene therapy? When should she tell the child the worst?

As a dilemma put to a group of European school pupils planning a career in scientific and medical research the question is hypothetical, but none the less an urgent one.

'The pace of development in genetics is so fast that we have to prepare in advance the scientists of tomorrow for the issues it will raise,' said Paolo Gallese, who led the Italian group from the Centre for Information, Education and Research on Science and Society in Milan.

Stefano Visinovi, 18, thought the baby should be born and allowed to get on with life: 'Your physical proportions are not a danger to health.' Some of his peers felt the child might suffer psychological problems, making him or her a legitimate target for gene therapy.

The debates, held at London's Science Museum, were a prelude to the European Week for Scientific Culture, an EU-sponsored series of more than 20 events at the end of last month, designed to examine and enhance public understanding of science and technology.

Genetic issues proved to be the hot topic, with a conference on biotechnology at The Hague, a forum on plant genetics at the Max Planck Institute in Cologne, and ethical debates at the Eksperimentarium centre in Copenhagen.

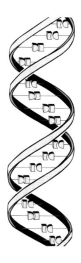

These initiatives follow a declaration by the World Health Organisation last month that the teaching of medical ethics should start in the classroom, be a compulsory part of every medical undergraduate's curriculum and, if possible, continue throughout the medical professional's life. It recommended that national associations should collaborate with schools.

Recent breakthroughs will enhance such initiatives, according to Hannu Salmi, leader of the Finnish delegation and the director of educational science at Helsinki's Heureka centre, Scandinavia's largest modern science facility.

These include the isolation of the gene that leads to haemophilia, heralding a cure which would obviate the need for increasingly risky blood transfusions. In Milan surgeons are set to treat by gene therapy a patient with a brain tumour, and across the Atlantic the first successful gene therapy has been performed on a four-year-old girl suffering from ADA deficiency, a disorder that impairs the immune system.

Nina Hautamaki, a Finnish student whose aunt has the disease, hopes that a genetic cure will be found in her lifetime. But she is not so happy about germ-line therapy – the alteration of genes in the sex cells, which would pass the 'correction' down the generations. This was the subject that most united the participants, with more than two-thirds against the idea and the remainder saying it would be acceptable only under certain strict conditions.

There was also a consensus on the value of food biotechnology. Given the choice between a tasty tomato that had been genetically tampered with and a watery 'natural' one, most would opt for the tasty one.

The most heated debate was over the public availability of information about individuals' genetic profiles. Should insurance companies be able to demand such information? Would you want to know if you were destined to develop breast cancer or cystic fibrosis? There is increasing scope for abuse of such information.

In contrast to the public's scepticism about genetic manipulation almost all the participants felt it was for the general good. Fabiana Gambarin, 18, from Italy, felt that public opinion was influenced too much 'by science-fiction films and scare stories in the media. They think it's far more dangerous than it is.'

It is these young people who will have to deal with the issues at the sharp end. According to Salmi: 'Too many decisions are made by middle-aged politicians. They won't be around to see the consequences of their decisions. The under-20s will and must be given as much opportunity as possible to discuss the possibilities.'

Genetic modification programmes and food use

From the National Consumer Council

Is it ethical?

Roger Straughan, in his paper for NCC,[1] discusses the objections to genetic modification. Many of these arguments are based on the assumption that such modification is 'intrinsically wrong, regardless of the good or bad effects it may produce. Most of these arguments maintain that genetic manipulation is in some way "unnatural" and therefore wrong.' The main strands of these arguments are:

- genetic manipulation involves 'playing God' by tinkering with the stuff of life;
- genetic manipulation assumes a 'reductionist' view of life encouraging us to adopt the chemist's perspective and look upon all forms of life as 'just DNA';
- genetic manipulation breaches barriers and boundaries between species which 'nature' has set up through the process of evolution to prevent genetic interactions between species. Or that GM programmes breach the 'creationist' view that all existing species were created once and for all by God and that to attempt to modify this arrangement constitutes a form of blasphemy. Both perspectives see species as 'sacred' and genetic manipulation as a violation of this 'sacredness';
- genetic manipulation distorts mankind's relationship with the rest of nature. By engineering plants and animals for our own purposes, we come to assume that we own other life-forms;
- genetic manipulation of animals involves 'unnatural' experiments and can cause suffering. And if human genes are transferred to animals, what human attributes, potentialities and rights might go with them?

National **Consumer** Council

- genetic manipulation could represent the first step on a slippery slope that leads inexorably to a nightmare programme of universal 'eugenics'.

These are the most often mentioned 'ethical' concerns about genetic modification.

> *Many of these arguments are based on the assumption that such modification is 'intrinsically wrong, regardless of the good or bad effects it may produce*

Roger Straughan concludes, however, that some of these arguments can be countered: for example, it is argued that: 'man has always "played God" and practised "eugenics" in his attempts to "improve" breeds of animal and strains of plants for his own ends. Genetic manipulation can be seen, therefore, as merely a more efficient and speedy method of doing what man has always tried to do. The emotive overtones of the word "eugenics"

should not lead us to assume that applying this method to the production of plants and animals will inevitably lead to a "genetically controlled society".'

In the context of transgenic programmes, however, is it not the case that many of the developments would/could not take place through 'selective breeding'? Are the complexity of technology and the speed with which developments happen now enabling 'science' to move further than is 'natural'? Could this mark the 'cut-off' point for consumers?

Some of the arguments put forward by the 'anti' groups, it is argued, rest on shaky foundations and obscure concepts, often presented in an emotive form. Nevertheless, it is clearly possible to hold coherent religious or metaphysical beliefs which require the rejection of genetic manipulation on moral and/or theological grounds. Roger Straughan continues: 'perhaps the most compelling of these concern the "reductionist" objection and the unease about patenting life forms – and it is interesting to note that these place less weight upon the intrinsic "wrongness" of genetic manipulation than upon the possible psychological effects it might produce on those who practise it.'

The range of beliefs outlined here are not held only by members of fringe or extreme minority groups. In a 1991 Eurobarometer study, 20 per cent of respondents found the genetic modification of animals totally unacceptable on moral grounds, while a further 28 per cent felt it should be considered on a case-by-case basis.[2]

So we can accept that such 'ethical' arguments feature very strongly in the arsenal of a large proportion of people. But are they consumer arguments, in the traditional sense of the word? Are they issues which the NCC should be seeking to voice? Is it the role of a consumer organisation to press such ethical concerns; what role should industry/government itself have in determining the 'ethics' of such developments? Can we devolve decisions on such grounds to a permanent standing committee on ethics?

● The above is an extract from *Genetic modification programmes and food use*, produced by the National Consumer Council. See page 39 for address details.

References

1 National Consumer Council, *The genetic manipulation of plants, animals and microbes: the social and ethical issues for consumers – a discussion paper*, Dr Roger Straughan, August 1989.

2 Commission of the European Communities, *Highlights of the Preliminary Results of the Spring 1991 Eurobarometer*, DGX11, Concertation Unit for Biotechnology in Europe, 1991.

'Frankenfood' scientists told: don't play God

By Geraint Smith

Scientists were warned today that opposition is strong to genetically engineered 'Frankenfood' – vegetable crops altered by the use of animal genes.

According to the first National Consensus Conference on Plant Biotechnology, tissue of animal origin is used in large-scale production of genetic material to modify plants. The aim is to improve taste and resistance to disease and give vegetables a longer shelf-life

But some people consider the incorporation of animal genes into plants to be 'playing God' and that the use of human genes in foodstuffs would be 'tantamount to cannibalism'.

The panel went on: 'There are many moral problems raised by plant biotechnology.'

Vegetarians and some religious faiths, especially the Jewish and Islamic religion, might find the use of pork and other animal genes to be unacceptable, they added.

'Sections of the community will intuitively feel plant biotechnology is morally wrong. This may well conflict with the philosophy of the scientific community.'

There was a moral obligation on producers to label foods which incorporate these genes, said the panel. 'Meaningful labelling is essential to allow vegetarians and people with religious objections to avoid products offensive to them. Bio-technology is established largely in the developed world and we need to recognise that our philosophies are different from those in less developed countries. The ethics and priorities of the peoples of developing countries also need to be taken into account before we pass judgement on their behalf.'

The comments come in the report to the conference – organised by the Science Museum – of a panel set up to act as a lay jury on biotechnology. A cross-section of 16 people, ranging from senior managers to teachers and cleaners, were given an intensive course in the latest thinking, research and practice of biotechnology.

They were then allowed to call as witnesses some of the country's leading scientists, policy-makers, plant-breeders, wholesalers and environmentalists.

Most genetic material currently used to modify plants is taken from bacteria and fungi. But experiments are known to be under way using genetic material from insects. The panel said benefits of biotechnology included less need for pesticides and the development of vegetable-based plastics and oils. But engineered genes could transfer between species to produce super-weeds, or bacteria could be freed which may disrupt weather patterns.

© *The Evening Standard November, 1995*

The concerns

From the Food and Drink Federation

Is it safe?

Opponents of genetic modification argue that we do not know enough about the science and that altering genes could lead to unforeseen problems for future generations.

Against that it is argued that strict controls do exist. In addition, since only the specific genes for a trait are identified and copied, the technology is far more precise than the trial-and-error approach of traditional plant and animal breeding.

What laws exist?

In the UK, the Food Safety Act requires that all food must be fit for consumption, i.e., must not be injurious to health, be unfit or contaminated. An additional set of safeguards controls the use of genetic modification in foods or food ingredients. These foods are assessed by a number of committees of independent experts, some of which include consumer representatives:

- The Advisory Committee on Novel Foods and Processes (ACNFP)
- The Committee on Toxicity of Chemicals in Food, Consumer Products and the Environment (COT)
- The Food Advisory Committee (FAC)

The Annual Reports of these Committees are a useful starting-point for those who wish to check if, and how, issues of concern are being addressed.

At European level a regulation that will harmonise procedures for the approval of all novel foods, including those produced using modern biotechnology, is under discussion. The UK procedures are already more developed than those in most other European countries and are expected to provide a blueprint for the European scheme.

What about the environment?

A main concern is that copy genes incorporated into a plant could 'escape' and transfer to another species with unwanted consequences. For example, it is argued that herbicide-resistant crops could cross-pollinate with weeds and so become herbicide-resistant themselves. Thus 'superweeds' could be created.

Some consumers and farmers are also concerned that making crops herbicide-resistant might lead to an increase in herbicide use, as the crops could withstand higher doses.

Supporters of biotechnology argue that stringent rules exist to safeguard against these possibilities and that the development of genetically modified plants will mean a decrease in the use of environmentally unfriendly herbicides.

What laws exist?

UK regulations which implement European Directives, control laboratory experiments, field trials and commercial use:

- The 'Genetically Modified Organisms (Contained Use) Regulations 1992'
- The 'Genetically Modified Organisms (Deliberate Release) Regulations 1992'

In the UK, the regulatory bodies are the Health and Safety Executive and the Department of the Environment.

Extensive risk-assessment trials are also being carried out in various countries to assess the environmental impact of releasing genetically modified plants.

The UK procedures are already more developed than those in most other European countries

---

Again, the Annual Reports of these bodies are a useful starting-point for those who wish to check if, and how, issues of concern are being addressed.

As with the subject of safety, it will remain important that consumer groups continue to be informed and to play a part in the decision-making process.

Who should own the rights?

Patent laws protect inventions for a fixed number of years. During this period no one else can copy or use the invention without permission, which usually has to be paid for. Should patent protection extend to genetic modification of foods?

The case for:
- Patent protection enables inventors to recoup their considerable investments in research and development; without it, far less research funding would be available.
- A prerequisite of patent protection is that the details of the patent must be published. Without patent protection, more inventions would be kept secret, which would slow up the development of the science.

The case against:
- Genes are not 'inventions' and therefore should not be subject to patent rights.
- It is wrong that our food supplies could be controlled by the few who can afford the development costs. Food should be available to all.

The UK National Consensus Conference on Plant Biotechnology, held in the autumn of 1994, recognised the need to protect inventors' investments, but felt that the current law needs some amendment.

The debate is set to continue.

Will developing countries benefit?

The case for:
- Crops could be especially adapted to the diverse farming conditions and practices, and offer greater nutritional value and a higher income.
- Energy-producing crops could also save natural resources and so conserve the environment.

The case against:
- Genetically modified products could reduce the developed countries' reliance on crops from developing countries. This could result in loss of trade and severe economic damage.
- Others doubt whether developing countries will actually receive the benefits.

These issues raise important political, ethical and trade questions which are not unique to modern biotechnology. They must be resolved at governmental and intergovernmental level to make sure that everyone benefits from the new technology.

What about labelling?

Labelling is an important way of keeping consumers informed about specific products. Where the use of modern biotechnology substantially changes the composition of the food, its nutritional properties, or the way it is used, there is a strong argument in favour of labelling.

If this is not the case, the argument is less clear cut: there is a limit to the amount of information that can realistically be put on a food label and there are other ways of providing such information to consumers.

A European perspective

This issue has also been considered at European level. The European Commission set up a Group of Advisers on the Ethical Implications of Biotechnology which delivered its opinion in May 1995.

The opinion stated that:
- Consumers must be provided with appropriate and understandable information which should be useful, possible to verify and not misleading.

- Labelling would be appropriate when modern biotechnology caused a substantial change in composition, nutritional value or the use for which the food was intended. The new composition and characteristics of the food, and the process, should be indicated.
- Consumers should be given a clear indication of where additional information can be obtained, especially when cultural and religious considerations arise.
- Producers and/or retailers should provide educational materials and access to state-of-the-art information networks, to complement the information provided on the label.

The food industry is now in discussion with consumer groups throughout Europe to find practical ways of meeting these needs.

Is it ethical?

Most people find the idea of genetically modifying plants acceptable, although some people disagree with all genetic modification on the grounds that we should not tamper with nature.

There is also concern about the possibility of transferring genes of animal or human origin to other animal species and plants.

However, the current consensus among scientists is that whilst the use of human copy genes in food production is theoretically possible, in practice it is very unlikely to be pursued. The use of animal copy genes in plants is more likely, but still very much dependent on consumer acceptance.

The Polkinghorne Committee

The UK Government set up a committee to consider these points, chaired by The Reverend Dr John Polkinghorne. It found that:
- Most Christian and Jewish groups in general find genetic modification acceptable;
- Muslims, Sikhs and Hindus have ethical objections to consuming organisms containing copy genes from animals which are the subject of dietary restrictions for their religion;
- Strict vegetarians would object to incorporating copy genes of animal origin in a plant.

The Committee recommended that, should this happen, clear labelling would be required to allow these groups to make an informed choice.

Animal welfare

Related to ethical issues are questions of animal welfare. Consumers are concerned that increasing yields from animals or adapting them to tolerate different environments could lead to distress for the animal.

In addition, animal welfare supporters stress that mankind has a moral obligation to care for animals and to honour their intrinsic value. It is therefore essential that all animal production, whether or not it involves modern biotechnology, clearly meets recognised standards of animal welfare.

Conclusion

Some of the concerns outlined in this article can be resolved by making more facts available to consumers. Others are more a matter of opinion and need to be discussed further.

The biotechnology debate, involving governments, scientists, industry and consumer groups, has already begun. Further wide-ranging and open discussions must continue so that all concerns can be properly addressed. Only then can we all benefit from the massive potential of new technology.

- The above is an extract from *Food for our Future – Food and Biotechnology*, produced by the Food and Drink Federation. See page 39 for address details.

© The Food and Drink Federation

Ethical questions on your dinner plate

Derek Burke offers an example of the kind of issue in the modern world about which the public is concerned and to which scientists need to be sensitive

This is a story about public perception, ethics, and the introduction of certain products of biotechnology for food use. It stems from my experience in chairing the Advisory Committee on Novel Foods and Processes (ACNFP): one of the network of committees that advise Government ministers. There are 18 members – experts in fields such as food microbiology or genetic modification – plus a consumer representative and an ethical adviser. We meet four times a year to consider a whole variety of new products and processes that come from the food industry.

By asking a series of 'what if?' questions we try to think of anything and everything that could go wrong, and then whether we can ensure that it won't, before offering our advice. We often go back to the company for more information or new experiments before making a final decision.

Four years ago, we were asked about sheep modified to carry the human gene for Factor IX, a protein involved in blood-clotting required for the treatment of haemophiliacs. The purpose of the research programme was to develop a cheaper and safer source of the factor, currently obtained from human blood. The gene was introduced by injection into the fertilised egg before reimplantation and rearing. It is present in all the cells of the animal, but not active in all of them; in this case the protein is released only into the animal's milk, from which it is readily purified.

The process is, however, not very efficient. In many cases, the injected gene does not integrate and is degraded. In others the gene is present, but not in a form which can work. So a large number of animals,

often over 100, are reared to obtain one animal which produces Factor IX in high yield.

We were asked what should happen to those animals which either contained no gene and were therefore absolutely normal, or which contained an inactive foreign gene or part of a gene. Could they be eaten?

We could not think of any reason why animals without any foreign DNA should not be eaten. But were newspapers going to run the headline 'Failures from genetic engineering in your supermarket' if we said yes? What about the animals containing an inactive human gene?

Was this just a stretch of DNA like any other? Or was it special, because it came from a human being?

> *Why do people think that some of these new developments are not only unwise, but wrong?*

Would people object to eating an animal containing a human gene? Would Muslims or Jews be concerned about pork genes in lamb, and vegetarians about animal genes in plants? We did not know, but decided it was a wider issue than one of pure technical safety, and suggested to the minister that a study group be established to consider the question. This was done, and its report was published last year (*Report of the Committee on the Ethics of Genetics Modification and Food Use*, HMSO).

But why were we so sensitive about the issue? First, the expert process – e.g. the work of ACNFP – is no longer trusted as it was. The man in the white laboratory coat no longer has the authority he once had – and has disappeared from advertisements as a consequence. He no longer recommends washing powder; the consumer does. Partly because experts have sometimes been wrong, and partly because we now realise that any so-called technical decisions have societal and environmental implications. Such decisions need opening up; and all expert committees, including ACNFP, are changing to meet this need. We publish the agenda for our meetings, and our advice to ministers; we have a press conference to introduce our annual report, and consumer and ethical-issues members of our committee.

Second, the general attitude to risk has changed. A hundred years ago the main objective was survival. Now we are much more concerned with the quality of life, and take survival for granted. We want a risk-free environment – especially if others take the decisions about the risk.

Third, we now understand that such risk decisions are not purely technical. We use other criteria besides risk/benefit judgements: outrage (how dare they do this); dread (the way many would feel about the risk of a nuclear-power-station accident); stigma (the label now attached to food irradiation).

Fourth, we weigh risk/benefit judgements differently in medicine and in food. Society has accepted biotechnology much more readily in medicine than in food. We use genetically modified micro-organisms to produce interferon, growth hormone or insulin – all in use in modern medicine – whereas there has been great resistance to the introduction of somatostatin to increase milk yields from cattle. When we are ill, and especially seriously ill, we will accept quite high levels of risk.

Then there is a series of ethical and moral issues. Why do people think that some of these new developments are not only unwise, but wrong?

A common complaint is that scientists are playing God. People say we have been breeding plants and animals for thousands of years, but moving genes across species barriers is unnatural and wrong. How do you know you are not going to release a new plague? Scientists reply that they see living systems as a unity, knowing that cells, from bugs to man, work in much the same way. So why shouldn't they move genes around? What is needed, says the scientist, is a clearer explanation of the science, and then people will be reassured.

That is fine, but sometimes misses the point – rather like raising one's voice, in English, to explain a point which an intelligent but non-English-speaking Frenchman has failed to grasp. Is there a danger that we fail to understand each other because we are talking different languages – and, more specifically, because we have different value-systems?

All parties agree that there are safety issues in, say, the genetic modification of crops. Scientists judge those issues on purely technical grounds; but that excludes those other issues – such as outrage, dread and stigma – which are part of the societal decision-making process.

This failure to talk about all the issues leads to misunderstanding and suspicion by the public. We scientists have got to listen, and try to deal with their concerns, not just say the same things in a louder voice.

Then there is the natural/unnatural issue. Some think that it is unwise, even unethical, to disturb the natural world – and that genetic modification is unnatural because it crosses species barriers. As a Christian, I do not accept that all that is natural is best; the world is not perfect, the original creation has been spoiled, and Christian faith deals with this robustly and straightforwardly. Christians too carry responsibility as stewards of the world; but the issues are of care and renewal rather than resistance to all change. Natural is not always best: fungal infection of crops with production of the ergot alkaloids is certainly not for the good of those who eat the crops.

Science too, I believe, must be less assertive, perhaps less arrogant, than is currently sometimes the case

---

There is another issue. Crudely, would eating sheep meat containing a single human gene, in among 100,000 sheep genes, be cannibalism – or if not cannibalism, offensive and ethically objectionable? Surely not. After all, a human gene is no more than a DNA sequence, like any other gene. It is not even the original gene – but a copy of that gene, copied more than ten-to-the-power-of-fifty times in the preparation process, before injection into the fertilised egg. So there is no more chance of eating the original human gene than of recovering a specific drop of water from all the oceans of the world. Indeed, the gene, once its sequence is known, can be made completely in the test-tube. Would people object to eating a completely synthetic human gene, which had never been near a human cell?

We found that people are uneasy about even this. Why? Partly, I think because they do not know where to draw the line between one gene and a thousand. Is this the start of a slippery slope? Partly also, I suggest, because people think there is something special about human genes. Is there a concern about what science is doing to our perception of humanness? People are loving, caring, choosing human beings, with deeply held beliefs and values, many of which are central to their view of what a human being is. They accept the centrality of our genes – but not that we are no more than a bunch of genes. So they think there must be something special about human genes, which must not be treated merely as chemicals.

Is this a reaction to reductionism – a rejection of the idea that we are nothing but a bunch of genes? The concern of the public is not lessened by the aggressive determination of some current biologists, or the slant of some of the science-education initiatives.

It is certainly a warning to Christians, and to all who hold a supernatural view of the world: that in stressing the underlying simplicity and order of our complex world which modern molecular biology reveals, and in stressing the power and effectiveness of modern technology, we must also stress the limits. Science too, I believe, must be less assertive, perhaps less arrogant, than is currently sometimes the case. We who are Christians have a special responsibility; for we are at ease with a God who is both personal and knowable and also creator and sustainer. We have a responsibility in our science, and in the public use of science, not to oversell, not to dismiss fears and concerns of others too lightly, and to be as even-handed as we can in our dealing with both the public and our own scientific community.

● Professor Derek C. Burke is Vice-Chancellor of the University of East Anglia. This article is a shortened version of the first Donald McKay lecture, given at the University of Keele during the British Association meeting there in September 1993.

© Church Times
July, 1994

What's on tomorrow's menu?

How would you feel about sitting down to a Sunday lunch of pork fortified with human genes or genetically engineered potatoes? It may sound like science fiction, but this could become fact. The food on tomorrow's dinner plate may owe more to a team of scientists than to farmers or horticulturalists

By Tim Lobstein and Anne Montague

Genetic engineering is the latest technology to hit the food industry and one that looks set to create a mini revolution. For years farmers and biologists have been giving nature a helping hand by selective breeding – mating a pig that is a good breeder with one that produces lean meat to produce a leaner pig that has lots of piglets.

But now, science has moved on so quickly that much more is possible. The question is, has genetic engineering of our food already gone too far? Do ordinary shoppers understand – or even know – if and how the food they're buying has been tampered with?

Transgenics is the practice of taking genes for individual characteristics, growth or fertility for example, from one living thing and inserting them into another. This enables scientists to produce a plant or animal with exactly the characteristics they want. Scientists can now cross the barriers between species – they can implant fish genes into tomatoes and cattle genes into chickens, producing plants or animals which then pass on the characteristics to their offspring.

In Britain and the US multinational food and genetic engineering companies are investing millions in producing more 'Frankenfoods', as the Americans have nicknamed them.

How will it affect our food?

Adding extra genes or tinkering with the existing ones won't usually affect the taste – so chicken genes in potatoes won't leave you with chicken-flavoured chips – unless the genes for affecting flavour have been engineered.

Transgenics can offer practical improvements. By taking a gene from the flounder, a fish that can survive in bitterly cold water, and inserting it into tomatoes, scientists have produced frost-resistant tomatoes which can be frozen and then thawed without losing their shape or consistency.

There's also the potential to develop healthier foods. An American company is working on potatoes for low-fat chips by adding a gene to potatoes to give them a higher starch content, which will make them less absorbent to the fat when fried. Work is also progressing on genetically altered coffee which has less caffeine and a better flavour even than normal coffee.

Some changes could reduce the need for additives and preservatives and keep food fresher for longer. Flavr Savr® – tomatoes genetically engineered to stay firm and fresh for longer by 'turning off' the gene that produces softening – have already been test marketed in the US, although resistance from consumer groups and a boycott by top chefs has meant they have been left in the greenhouses to rot.

Down on the farm

For farmers and food companies genetic engineering could mean increased productivity, lower costs – and huge profits.

US genetic engineering companies have produced new strains of peanuts, cucumbers, potatoes and tomatoes resistant to the viruses which attack the growing plants.

Scientists have engineered a form of sugar beet which is resistant to caterpillar attack by introducing genes from bacteria that make a caterpillar toxin. The race is on to engineer low-maintenance, high-productivity animals too. The future may see us buying giant chickens, fortified with cattle growth genes, and pork containing human genes to produce bigger animals and leaner meat.

Dr John Webb of the Cotswold Pig Development Company predicts that eventually pork meat might be grown without the need for pigs, while scientists at Newcastle University are working on the world's first vegetarian pig! These pigs could be fed on grass, making them cheaper and more convenient for farmers to manage.

Genetic engineering could offer great potential for feeding the world's starving millions too, by producing crops that are disease-resistant and able to survive drought and salty conditions.

Unfortunately, research so far has concentrated on improving the agricultural crops of the developed world, rather than on the staple foods of developing countries.

Some experts believe that genetic engineering may actually harm developing countries by producing cheaper substitutes that will eliminate the need for their exports.

Cane sugar, a staple export for several developing countries, is fast being replaced in the West by high-fructose corn syrup produced from maize starch using genetic engineering.

Can we trust scientists?

All of this sounds too good to be true – so what's the catch? Safety is one concern. Food and genetic engineering companies insist that genetically engineered foods will be as safe as those from conventional breeding methods and may even be safer and healthier than foods grown using chemical pesticides and fertilisers. But the reality is that we just don't know – genetic engineering leads to combinations that would never occur naturally and could have unforeseen consequences. Government checks should ensure safety, but today's consumers will still be the guinea pigs who 'test' this new generation of foods without any say as to whether or not they should be available.

The expression 'you are what you eat' may prove chillingly accurate if some of the products of genetic engineering end up on our dinner plates. A pharmaceutical company in Edinburgh recently applied to the Ministry of Agriculture Fisheries and Food (MAFF) to send its surplus sheep to the abattoir. The sheep had been part of a group bred using human genes to produce milk containing medically valuable proteins. It was possible that they contained human genes and, in a sense, their meat could be partly human. MAFF refused the licence and set up the Polkinghorne Committee to examine the ethics of mixing species and selling the results for human consumption. The Committee's

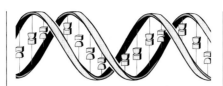

conclusions were, according to Steve Emmott of the Committee on Biotechnology and Food (COBAF) – an alliance of concerned environmental, consumer, trade unions and animal welfare organisations – 'a recipe for gene fudge. The Committee set no limits on what industry could do,' says Emmott.

Public confidence has not been boosted by secrecy surrounding the first generation of genetically engineered organisms (GEOs). The genetically engineered milk-boosting hormone bovine somatotropin (BST) – produced from genetically modified bacteria – was secretly tested in the UK for four years and the resulting milk added to our milk supply without being labelled in any way, despite pressure from consumer groups to do so.

Is the consumer protected?

Food producers must, by law, provide food that is safe to eat. Although all additives, colourings, preservatives and processing agents have, by law, to go before the Government's Food Advisory Committee, there are no legal requirements about foods containing GEOs. Companies can submit foods to the Government's Advisory Committee on Novel Foods and Processes (ACNFP) for examination and tests and, in practice, most do, but this is entirely voluntary. Critics want more statutory controls on companies releasing new foods, and a more rigorous testing system.

Britain has no binding rules about the labelling of genetically modified foods, just guidelines recommending that certain foods – those containing human genes, plant foods containing animal genes and any food containing genes from religiously significant animals like pigs or cows – should carry explanatory labels.

What is needed now?

COBAF are campaigning for tougher controls on the genetic engineering of food, with a tighter rein on the release of GEOs and proper labelling

of all genetically engineered foods.

Professor Moseley, acting director of the Institute of Food Research, and a member of the ACNFP believes that consumer opinion will play a powerful part in determining which foods reach our dinner plates. 'The consumer holds the key to everything,' he says. 'It's up to ordinary people to make their voices heard.' Retailers and food manufacturers do respond to public pressure. The Co-op recently became the first retailer to back the customer's right to know what they are eating, by labelling vegetarian cheese containing genetically engineered chymosin which is used to curdle it. (Chymosin is present in the rennet of calves' stomachs, but in this form is unsuitable for vegetarians.) They have also given a guarantee to label all Co-op products known to contain genes from non-related species. They have also refused to stock food containing human genes and guaranteed that Co-op products won't use vegetables or fruits containing animal genes.

Farmers are already talking of transgenic featherless chickens that don't need plucking and sheep that shed their wool without shearing. And perhaps someone will combine a cocoa plant with a spinach plant or a Brussels sprout giving us chocolate-flavoured greens, a parent's dream. Where such dreams are, science isn't very far behind.

What can you do?

Educate yourself on the issues surrounding genetic engineering. For further information contact Genetics Forum, 3rd Floor, 5/11 Worship Street, London EC2A 2BH. The Food Commission, (0171) 628 7774, publish the quarterly *Food Magazine* which has regular updates on GEO foods.

Write to your MP and MEP (many important developments will be regulated at EC level). Give them your views about the genetic modification of food and ask for their support on food labelling.

Write to your supermarket and ask for their policy on stocking and labelling GEO products and BST milk. © *Living Magazine June, 1994*

Letters to the editor

Human genes: patently not the case

Sir: Your report today on the rejection of the European Biotechnology Directive by the European Parliament suggests that the biotechnology industry is disappointed with the outcome. In my experience, both as a patent attorney representing various biotechnology companies and as a member of the Industrial Property Advisory Committee of the Bioindustry Association, that is not the case: the industry is in general pleased that the directive was rejected. What had started out in 1988 as a moderately useful but hardly essential tidying-up exercise in a difficult area of law subsequently became a vehicle for special-interest groups to undermine the growing and established case-law which permits the patenting of proteins, DNA and other entities important to the biotechnology industry. Although industry could have lived with the rather tortured compromise wording eventually put to the European Parliament, frankly there was something of a sigh of relief when the whole package was rejected. The law can now continue its largely harmonised development in a manner that promotes and balances the interests both of the industry and of the consumers who will ultimately benefit from its efforts.

Yours faithfully,
A. G. SHEARD
Kilburn & Strode Patent Attorneys
London WC1

Sir: It is incorrect to suggest in your article 'MEPs reject gene patenting' (2 March) that the decision of the European Parliament to reject the European Biotechnology Directive marks an end to the possibility of securing patent protection in Europe for human genes or cells. The European Patent Office (a non-EU body to which all EU members subscribe) has granted several patents relating to human genes and, indeed, recently upheld such a patent despite a legal challenge that it was unethical. The EPO decides whether a gene can be patented on the basis of criteria which are applied to all types of invention, namely whether it is new, not obvious and has a practical use. The origin of the ill-fated directive lay in part as a response to concerns that different or additional criteria should apply to the patenting of human genes, in particular moral criteria. Although the EPO may also refuse patents on moral grounds, it has declined to do so where the invention relates to technologies that are both permitted and tightly regulated by other laws in member states. It is probably right in the long term that all inventions be assessed by the same criteria for patentability. These criteria can be traced back to the first UK patent law of 1624 and have been able to accommodate 20th-century industries in electronics and pharmacy. The EPO has proved capable of determining the patentability of biological inventions without the need of a special directive from Brussels, and this does provide some level of certainty for industry, which would have faced further confusion had the directive been passed.

Yours faithfully,
ADRIAN BRASNETT
London N16

A patent need to look at ethics

Sir: Your two patent lawyer correspondents (Letters, 4 March), writing in response to the news that the European Parliament has rejected the EU directive on patenting life-forms, both seek to portray the decision as being of little consequence for the biotechnology industry. This is curiously at odds with the furious lobbying that was going on in Brussels up to the last moment and the appearance of industry representatives on TV and radio arguing that rejection would sound the death-knell for future investment in Europe. There is no doubt that deep issues are raised by the creation of new genetically engineered plants and animals and the possibility of genetic manipulation of living human material. One MEP put his finger directly on the problem when he said in the debate that, until we got a satisfactory consensus of opinion on the ethics of biotechnology, it was simply inappropriate to grant private commercial monopolies on genetic material. What we need is a cool look at what is, and what is not, acceptable to society in the use of this technology. Our MEPs have created the opportunity for this to happen. If industry presses on regardless with *ad hoc* patent applications, it will run into the same determined opposition that blocked the directive.

Yours faithfully,
STEVE EMMOTT
Patent Concern Coalition
The Genetics Forum
London EC2

Ancient law and modern science

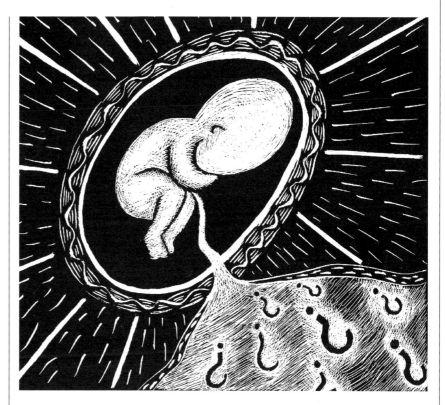

During the early eighties, Britain had its great debate on the sanctity of human life, the status of the human embryo, and what it was permissible for scientists to do with human beings and with human reproduction. The debate was sparked by the birth in 1978 of Louise Brown, the world's first test-tube baby. Concern over the ethical implications of the new 'reproductive technologies' led the Government to establish a committee chaired by Mary (now Baroness) Warnock to set the limits of what was acceptable. The committee stimulated a structured public debate. Inchoate but powerful public concerns were reassured, not only by the measured and reasoned conclusions of the Warnock Committee's report, but also by the simple knowledge that the committee was examining such matters

But science does not stand still. IVF is, by the standards of the nineties, an 'old' technology. The forefront of today's research is manipulating human genes rather than embryos. Instead of transplanting organs, such as kidneys, doctors in Britain are already transplanting human genes into the bodies of those who suffer from inherited diseases such as cystic fibrosis. Later this week, the House of Commons Committee on Science and Technology will hear evidence on the 'new genetics' from representatives of the Jewish and Anglican religious traditions

Last week, the Nuffield Council on Bioethics produced a clear report on the legal and ethical issues surrounding the use of human organs and tissues in medicine and research. The study revealed that most laws relevant to biotechnology of the late 20th century are Victorian statutes designed to combat body-snatching

The council advocated that human bodies and body parts should not be anyone's 'property', nor should they be the subject of commercial transactions. Yet, for the past decade or more, human cell lines and human genes have been patented – have become the intellectual property of research institutes and companies.

These issues are too pressing to be ignored. The status of genes is central to the creation of children and of what it is to be human

---

Various groups have opposed such patents on the grounds that they are as unethical as patenting whole organs or surgical procedures. Meanwhile, defenders of the system believe that the development of new medicines would be handicapped if researchers and companies were deprived of the rewards for their work that the patent system offers. Whichever side is right, there is undeniable public and professional unease

These issues are too pressing to be ignored. The status of genes is central to the creation of children and of what it is to be human. The new genetics promise great benefits, but unless limits are set we could find ourselves with little say over a world in which babies can be designed and commercial interests intrude into the most intimate aspects of human relations.

That is why we need a full debate aimed at devising legislation to set rules governing a host of issues ranging from genetic testing and insurance to patenting, experimentation and confidentiality. The time has come to revisit the Warnock findings.

© *The Independent*
April, 1995

INDEX

abortion, and genetic
    engineering 20
agriculture, and biotechnology 5,
    6-7, 10, 15, 24, 31-2
animal welfare
    and genetic engineering 23, 25,
      26, 28, 31
    and transgenic farm animals 12
animals
    and organ transplants 11, 12,
      16-18
    transgenic 11-12, 14, 22-3, 26,
      32, 34, 35
    see also farm animals

babies, 'designer' 19
bacteria, creating man-made 13
biotechnology
    advantages and disadvantages 14
    and agriculture 5, 6-7, 10
    attitudes towards 5, 15
    defining 1
    ethics of 16-37
    food-related benefits 5, 6-7, 15
    knowledge of 2, 15
    and plant breeding 4-5, 6-7, 10
    public image of 1-2
    see also food biotechnology
breast cancer, and gene therapy
    20-1

cancer research, and gene therapy
    8, 20-1
chickens, genetically engineered
    11, 34
Christianity, and genetic
    modification 31, 33
Compassion in World Farming
    (CIWF) 26
crime, violent, and genetic
    fingerprinting 4
cystic fibrosis (CF) 19, 21, 22, 25,
    37

developing countries, and food
    biotechnology 31, 34-5
diet, and biotechnology 5
diseases
    cured by organ transplants 22
    diagnosis in farm animals 7
    laboratory models of 12
DNA (deoxyriboneuclic acid) 4, 23
    and cancer research 8
    creating man-made bacteria 13
    and gene therapy 19

and genetic fingerprinting 4
drought resistance 7

European Commission, and food
    biotechnology 31

farm animals 10
    disease diagnosis 7
    and genetic engineering 24
    genetic modification of 7, 14
    selective breeding of 34
    stress in pigs 7
    transgenic 11, 12, 14, 16-18,
      22-3, 26, 34, 35
    vaccines 7
food biotechnology 1, 2, 4, 5, 6-7
    and consumers 34, 35
    and developing countries 31
    ethics of 24, 25, 27, 28-35
    and the European Commission
      31
    labelling 31, 35
    laws regarding 30
    and patenting 30-1
    risk/benefit judgements in 32-3
    and safety 35
    see also plant biotechnology
Food and Drink Federation 5, 6-7,
    14, 15, 30-1

gene piracy 25
gene therapy 25, 37
    and cancer research 8
    defining 19
    ethics of 19-23, 27
    and transgenic animals 11, 12,
      22-3
genes 3, 19
genetic engineering
    ethics of 16-37
    and organ transplants 11, 12,
      16-18, 22-3
    public opinion on 10, 26, 27
genetic patenting 24-5, 30, 36
genetic screening 25, 27
genetic testing 25
Genetics Forum 24-5, 35, 36
GEOs (genetically engineered
    organisms) 35
GMOs (genetically manipulated
    organisms) 12

haemophilia, treatment of 11, 19, 32
homosexuality, and genetic
    engineering 19, 20

Human Genome Project (HGP) 3,
    9, 19, 23

Imperial Cancer Research Fund
    3, 8
insurance companies, and genetic
    screening 19, 21, 25, 27

medical ethics 27
micro-organisms 7

National Consumer Council 28-9
Nuffield Council on Bioethics 18,
    21, 37
nutritional value, and
    biotechnology 6

organ transplants
    ethics of 16-18
    and Islamic law 17
    and transgenic pigs 11, 12, 16-
      18, 22-3

patenting, genetic 24-5, 30, 36
pigs
    transgenic 11, 12, 16-18, 22-3,
      26
plant biotechnology 4-5, 6-7, 10
    and animal genes 29, 31, 32
    ethics of 24, 29, 30, 31, 33
    transgenic 34-5

religion, and genetic modification
    31, 33, 37

sheep, transgenic 11, 12, 32, 33, 35
stress, in farm animals 7

tomatoes, transgenic 1, 2, 6, 34
transgenic animals 11-12, 14, 22-3,
    26, 32, 34, 35
transplants *see* organ transplants

vaccines
    for farm animals 7
    production of 14
vegetarians, and food
    biotechnology 29, 31
viruses 13

Warnock Committee Report 37
weed control 6

xenotransplantation 11, 12, 16-18,
    22-3, 26

ADDITIONAL RESOURCES

You might like to contact the following organisations for further information. Due to the increasing cost of postage, many organisations cannot respond to enquiries unless they receive a stamped, addressed envelope.

Animal Aid
7 Castle Street
Tonbridge
Kent TN9 1BH
Tel: 01732 364546

Opposed to any use of animals in medical research.

BioIndustry Association
14-15 Belgrave Square
London SW1X 8PS
Tel: 0171 245 9911

Aims to foster greater public awareness and understanding of biotechnology and to encourage informed public debate about its development.

Biomedical Research Education Trust
58 Great Marlborough St
London W1V 1DD
Tel: 0171 287 2818

Supports the responsible use of animals in medical research. Leaflets, fact sheets, videos, speakers available.

Compassion in World Farming (CIWF)
Charles House
5a Charles Street
Petersfield
Hampshire GU32 3EH
Tel: 01730 268070

Campaigns against the genetic engineering of farm animals. They publish a fact sheet and report on the issue.

European Federation of Biotechnology
Research and Information Services
National Museum of Science and Industry
London SW7 2DD
Tel: 0171 938 8201
Fax: 0171 938 8213

Aims to foster greater public awareness and understanding of biotechnology and to encourage informed public debate about its development. Publishes a series of briefing papers.

Food Commission
102 Gloucester Place
London W1H 3DA
Tel: 0171 628 7774

Provides education, information, advice and research on nutrition, diet, health and food production. Runs various educational and research campaigns. Publishes *Food* magazine. Produces other publications.

Food & Drink Federation
6 Catherine Street
London WC2B 5JJ
Tel: 0171 836 2460

Produces publications and surveys on food and biotechnology.

Genetics Forum
3rd Floor
5-11 Worship Street
London EC2A 2BH
Tel: 0171 638 0606

A public interest group campaigning for the socially responsible use of genetic engineering. They publish a bulletin, *The Splice of Life*, ten times a year. Available on subscription.

Green Alliance
49 Wellington Street
London WC2E 7BN
Tel: 0171 836 0341
Fax: 0171 240 9205

Works to raise the prominence of the environment on the agendas of all key policy-making institutions in the UK. They have published a briefing document: *Why are environmental groups concerned about release of genetically modified organisms into the environment?*

Imperial Cancer Research Fund
PO Box 123
Lincoln's Inn Fields
London WC2A 3PX
Tel: 0171 242 0200
Fax: 0171 269 3262

Publishes series of publications on their work. Their free booklet, *Genes and Mankind*, provides a very useful account of the role genes play in human development, diversity and health.

Ministry of Agriculture, Fisheries and Food (MAFF)
Publications Department
London SE99 7TP
Tel: 0645 556000

Publish *Genetically Modified Food* (ask for Ref: 2052) in their Food Sense series. Publications are free but take up to ten days for delivery.

National Centre for Biotechnology Education
University of Reading
Department of Microbiology
Reading RG6 6AJ
Tel: 01734 873 743

Produce leaflets, fact sheets, a video and laboratory equipment. They also conduct courses.

National Consumers' Council
20 Grovenors' Gardens
London SW1W 0DH
Tel: 0171 730 3469

Set up by the Government in 1975 to act as an independent voice for domestic consumers in the UK.

Patent Concern
c/o Genetics Forum
3rd Floor
5-11 Worship Street
London EC2A 2BH
Tel: 0171 638 0606

An alliance of public interest groups opposed to the patenting of life-forms.

Royal Society for the Prevention of Cruelty to Animals (RSPCA)
Causeway
Horsham
West Sussex RH12 1HG
Tel: 01403 264181

Produces a wide range of leaflets and other materials on animal welfare issues. Please contact the Enquiries Service.

ACKNOWLEDGEMENTS

The publisher is grateful for permission to reproduce the following material.

Chapter One: Recent developments

Dispelling the monster myth, © University Life, August 1995, *Knowledge of biotechnology,* © The Food and Drink Federation, September 1995, *Genes and mankind,* © The Imperial Cancer Research Fund, 1995, *Biotechnology offers a safer, more secure world,* © The Financial Times, June 1994, *Attitudes to biotechnology,* © The Food and Drink Federation, September 1995, *The benefits of biotechnology,* © The Food and Drink Federation, *Gene therapy and cancer research,* © The Imperial Cancer Research Fund, *The only hope for dying children,* © Scotland on Sunday, April 1994, *Call for public support of genetic engineering,* © The Newcastle Journal, February 1994, *Pigs bred for human transplants,* © The Scotsman, March 1994, *Uses of genetically engineered animals,* © RSPCA Research Animals Department, *Genetics milestone,* © The Independent, *Potential advantages and disadvantages,* © RSPCA Research Animals Department, *Disadvantages of biotechnology,* © The Food and Drink Federation, *Biotechnology report,* © The Food and Drink Federation, September 1995.

Chapter Two: Right or wrong?

Four legs very good, © The Guardian, August 1995, *Ethics of heartless pigs,* © The Guardian, August 1995, *Engineering answers to question of genes,* © Scotland on Sunday, February 1994, *The moral maze,* © The Daily Mail, October 1994, *Transgenic pigs,* © The Daily Mail, September 1995, *Animal welfare implications of genetic engineering,* © RSPCA Research Animals Department, *Why worry about genetic engineering?,* © The Genetics Forum, September 1995, *Ethical implications of transgenic animal production,* © Compassion in World Farming, September 1995, *Facing up to gene genies of tomorrow,* © The European, December 1994, *Genetic modification programmes and food use,* © National Consumer Council, February 1993, *'Frankenfood' scientists told: don't play God,* © The Evening Standard, November 1995, *The Concerns,* © The Food and Drink Federation, *Ethical questions on your dinner plate,* © Church Times, July 1994, *What's on tomorrow's menu?,* © Living Magazine, June 1994, *Letters to the editor,* © The Independent, March 1995, *A patent need to look at the ethics,* © The Independent, March 1995, *Ancient law and modern science,* © The Independent, April 1995.

Photographs and Illustrations

Pages 1, 8, 20: Andrew Smith/Folio Collective, page 3: Anthony Haythornthwaite/Folio Collective, pages 4, 11, 21, 25, 29: Ken Pyne, pages 13, 15, 23, 34, 37: Katherine Fleming/Folio Collective.

Craig Donnellan
Cambridge
January, 1996